NEW SERMON OUTLINES

ROMANS
to
REVELATION

GORDON JONES

LOIZEAUX
Neptune, New Jersey

NEW SERMON OUTLINES
Romans to Revelation

© 1996 Gordon H. Jones

Originally published by CMML Publications, 1988
as *The Alliterated Outline of the Bible*.

A Publication of Loizeaux Brothers, Inc.
*A Nonprofit Organization Devoted to the Lord's Work
and to the Spread of His Truth*

Library of Congress Cataloging-in-Publication Data

Jones, Gordon (Gordon H.)
[Alliterated outline of the Bible. Selections]
New sermon outlines of the New Testament / by Gordon Jones.
Originally published as part of: The alliterated outline of the Bible.
CMML Publications. 1988.
Contents: [v. 1] Matthew to Acts—[v. 2] Romans to Revelation.
ISBN 0-87213-452-0 (pbk.: v. 1: alk. paper).—
ISBN 0-87213-453-9 (pbk.: v. 2: alk. paper).
1. Bible N.T.—Outlines, syllabi, etc. I. Title.
BS2525.J6625 1996
225'.02'02—dc20 96-1096

Printed in the United States of America

10 9 8 7 6 5 4 3 2 1

CONTENTS

PREFACE

It was the puritan Thomas Goodwin who said: "The Holy Spirit had great aims in writing Holy Scripture." This we may discover for ourselves in the study of the Word of God for which there is no substitute. If the following outlines encourage the reader to do this, the purpose will have been achieved. The notes that precede the outlines of each book have been gleaned through the years and may prove to be of help, especially to young believers.

I am sincerely grateful to my friend and colleague Mr. Alan Chambers for his painstaking perusal and detailed editing of the entire manuscript, without which these outlines would probably never have been published.

May the gracious Holy Spirit of God give illumination, direction, and power in service as a result of attention to our Lord's command: "Search the Scriptures."

GORDON H. JONES

ROMANS

NOTES

1. It is probable that the Gospel was first brought to Rome (the capital of the then known world) by those who had heard it in Jerusalem (Acts 2:10).
2. It appears that Paul had many friends in Rome before he went there, as chapter 16 suggests.
3. Paul had intended to visit Rome while at Ephesus (Acts 19:21).
4. There were probably more Gentiles than Jews in the church at Rome.
5. This Epistle is a systematic presentation of the plan of salvation through faith in the Lord Jesus Christ.
6. It is a masterly statement of the doctrine of justification by faith.
7. It answers Jewish objections when accepting the Gospel of the Lord Jesus Christ, about which the readers knew.
8. Note the fact that the first person singular "I" is mentioned more than thirty times in chapter 7 and the "Holy Spirit" is mentioned twenty times in chapter 8.

GENERAL OUTLINE

I.   DOCTRINE OF RIGHTEOUSNESS BY FAITH (1:1–11:36)
II. DEVELOPMENT OF RIGHTEOUSNESS BY FIDELITY (12:1–16:27)

DETAILED OUTLINE

I.   DOCTRINE OF RIGHTEOUSNESS BY FAITH (1:1–11:36)
   A. Commencement of the Discussion (1:1-17)
      1. Paul's Position Separated for the Lord's Service (1:1)
      2. Prophets Promised the Savior and His Good News (1:2)
      3. Process and Power Shown in Person of Christ (1:3-6)

4. Peace and Praise for the Saints at Rome (1:7-8)
5. Prayer and Prosperity for a Journey by Paul (1:9-10)
6. Purpose of the Proposed Visit to Them (1:11-13)
   a. Impart Some Spiritual Gift (1:11)
   b. Inform Himself about Them and They of Him (1:12)
   c. Intend Coming in spite of Setbacks (1:13)
7. Preaching and Progressing in the Work of the Lord (1:14-17)
   a. Duty to Preach Everywhere (1:14)
   b. Dedication in the Task of Doing So (1:15)
   c. Declaration regarding the Message (1:16)
   d. Doctrine, "The just shall live by faith" (1:17)
B. Condition of the World (1:18-3:20)
   1. Gentiles (1:18-32)
      a. Wrath Explained (1:18)
         (1) Against the Ungodly
         (2) Against the Unrighteous
      b. Without Excuse (1:19-20)
         (1) They Have Revelation
         (2) They Have Illustrations
         (3) They Have Creation
      c. Worldly Excesses Revealed As They Are (1:20-23)
         (1) No Knowledge of God
         (2) No Thanks
         (3) No Honor
         (4) No Humility
         (5) No Wisdom
         (6) No Perception
         (7) No Understanding
      d. Working Evil a Natural Propensity (1:24-27)
         (1) Result
         (2) Ruination
         (3) Retribution
      e. Worthy of Extinction (1:28-32)
         (1) Reprobate in spite of Knowledge (1:28)
         (2) Record of Indictment—Over Twenty Listed Sins (1:29-31)
         (3) Retribution Inevitable Thereafter (1:32)
   2. Jews (2:1-3:8)
      a. Involvement of All Israel (2:1-4)

        (1) Inexcusable
        (2) Incapable
        (3) Ignorant
    b. Impenitence of Israel (2:5-11)
        (1) Assessment
        (2) Actions
        (3) Alternatives
    c. Impartiality of the Judge (2:12-16)
        (1) Rule of Operation (2:12)
        (2) Response in Obedience (2:13)
        (3) Reward in the Offing (2:14-16)
            (a) Work
            (b) Witness
            (c) Wishfulness
    d. Instructions Offered to Offset (2:17-24)
        (1) Boasting (2:17-18)
        (2) Blindness (2:19-20)
        (3) Blasphemy (2:21-24)
    e. Identity of Israel with the Law (2:25–3:8)
        (1) Argument
        (2) Answer
        (3) Advantage
            (a) Privilege of Guardianship (3:1-2)
            (b) Proof of God's Goodness (3:3-6)
            (c) Plague of Gossipy-Slander (3:7-8)
3. Whole World (3:9-20)
    a. Sentence: "All under sin" (3:9-11)
        No Man with Right Standing or Understanding
    b. Senses: "All gone out of the way" (3:12-18)
        (1) Life
        (2) Mouth
        (3) Feet
        (4) Eyes
    c. Subjection: "All the world...guilty" (3:19-20)
        (1) Law Speaks to Edification
        (2) Law Silences Everyone
        (3) Law Specifies and Exposes Sin
C. Consolation and Comfort (3:21–8:39)
    1. Imputed Righteousness (3:21–5:21)
        a. Romans 3:21-31

(1) Righteousness of God a Fact for Faith (3:21-22)
(2) Ransom Required to Meet the Offence (3:23)
  (a) Nature of the Sinner
  (b) Need of the Sinner
(3) Remedy Provided for the Benefit of All (3:24-26)
  (a) Substitute Made Propitiation for Us
  (b) Sacrifice Made Justification Possible
(4) Result (3:27-31)
  (a) Forgiveness for Sinners
  (b) Fulfillment and Satisfaction for the Lord

b. Romans 4:1-25
(1) Demonstration by Faith of Abraham (4:1-4)
(2) Definition of Faith in Imputed Righteousness (4:5-8)
(3) Difference between the Signs and Signification (4:9-12)
(4) Dependence on Faith Alone—As Abraham, So We (4:13-17)
(5) Decision of Faith by Abraham to Believe (4:18-22)
(6) Design of Faith for Us All—"If we believe" (4:23-25)

c. Romans 5:1-21
(1) Acquittal—Justified by Faith (5:1)
(2) Access—To Grace and Rejoicing (5:2)
(3) Afflictions Bring Progress in Experience (5:3-5)
  (a) Patience in Relation to Others
  (b) Experience in Relation to Self
  (c) Hope in Relation to the Future
  (d) Love in Relation to Life
(4) Affection Brought Christ to Die for Us (5:6-8)
(5) Association Brings Security and the Saving Life of Christ (5:9-11)
(6) Antagonists Being the Old and New Natures (5:12-21)
  (a) Explanation (5:12-16)
  (b) Evidence (5:17-18)
  (c) Edification (5:19-21)

b. Intimations to Israel (10:5-10)
   (1) Verdict of the Law—Do and Live (10:5)
   (2) Voice of Grace—Live by Faith and Do (10:6-8)
   (3) Validity of Faith in Exercise of Heart (10:9-10)
   (4) Victory of Faith in Christ (10:11-13)
       (a) No Disappointment (10:11)
       (b) No Difference (10:12)
       (c) No Doubts (10:13)
c. Inquiry of Israel (10:14-25)
   (1) Features—How to Hear and Believe (10:14-15)
       (a) How to Hear the Word
       (b) How to Believe the Word
   (2) Frustration—Hard to Believe the Word
       (10:16,19,21)
   (3) Facts—Hearing the Word Brings Faith (10:17)
   (4) Found—Having Believed the Word (10:18,20)

3. Romans 11
   a. Foreknowledge of God regarding Israel (11:1-6)
      (1) Assurance of God's Purposes for Israel
          (11:1-2)
      (2) Attestation from the Old Testament Record
          (cf. 1 Kings 19) (11:2-4)
      (3) Argument according to Grace Not Works
          (11:5-6)
   b. Failure of Israel (11:7-11)
      (1) They Slumbered and Slept in Days of
          Opportunity (11:7-8)
      (2) They Stumbled, Snared by Their Lack of
          Understanding (11:9-11)
   c. Fruitfulness of Israel (11:12-18)
      (1) Riches of God Shared by Jew and Gentile
          (11:12-14)
      (2) Reconciliation of Jew and Gentile (11:15-16)
      (3) Root Which Bears the Branches and Feeds
          Them (11:17-18)
   d. Fear for Gentile Believers (11:19-22)
      (1) Separation because of Israel's Unbelief (11:19)
      (2) Standing by Faith Not Works (11:20)
      (3) Severity of God Calls for Humility (11:21-22)

      e. Fellowship Together (11:22-25)
- (1) Goodness of God Acknowledged (11:22)
- (2) Grafting Again of Israel No Problem (11:23)
- (3) Gentiles Now Enjoy the Blessings of God Too (11:24-25)

      f. Final Word about Israel (11:26-36)
- (1) Message concerning Israel for the Future (11:26-28)
- (2) Mercy of God Comes to All by Faith Alone (11:29-32)
- (3) Mind of God Commented On in Conclusion (11:33-36)

II. DEVELOPMENT OF RIGHTEOUSNESS BY FIDELITY (12:1–16:27)

  A. Romans 12:1-21

    1. Commitment to God (12:1-2)
- a. Plea of the Apostle to Believers (12:1)
- b. Presentation of the Body as a Living Offering (12:1)
- c. Proof of Dedication to God Shown (12:2)
  - (1) Conforming to the Will of God
  - (2) Transforming Mind and Life in Renewal

    2. Consecrated Service (12:3-8)
- a. Humility and Self-Examination Called For (12:3)
- b. Harmony in Serving Together As Equal Members (12:4-5)
- c. Heartwhole Service—Seven Gifts Mentioned (12:6-8)

    3. Consideration for Others (12:9-16)
- a. Examples of Love One toward Another Believer
- b. Enlightenment of Love Shown to All
- c. Energized by Love without Partiality

    4. Communicating to Unbelievers (12:17-21)
- a. Principles of Honest Living Stated (12:17)
- b. Peaceful Objective before Us All (12:18)
- c. Payment of Wrong Acts in His Hands (12:19)
- d. Progress of Overcoming Each Day (12:20-21)

  B. Romans 13:1-14

    1. Regarding the Duty Owed to Those over Us (13:1-5)

F. Romans 16:1-26
   1. Bearer of the Letter (16:1-2)
      a. Sister in the Lord—Phoebe (16:1)
      b. Servant of the Lord at Cenchrea (16:1)
      c. Succorer of the Lord's Servants (16:2)
   2. Brotherly Love to So Many (16:3-16,21-23)
   3. Burden of Loyalty to the Word (16:17-20)
      a. Discernment of Error When It Appears (16:17-18)
      b. Defence of the Truth When It Is Assailed (16:17-18)
      c. Dedication of Believers in and to the Truth (16:19-20)
   4. Benediction in the Lord's Name (16:24,27)
      a. Message of the Man in This Book the Lord's (16:24,27)
      b. Manifestation of the Mystery of Salvation from the Lord (16:25-26)

1 Corinthians

Notes

1. It is probable that this Epistle was written by Paul while on his second missionary journey with Silas.
2. It was probably written about A.D. 57.
3. It appears that this was not the first letter Paul had written to the Corinthian believers (1 Corinthians 5:9).
4. News had reached Paul of some disorders in the church at Corinth. This letter was written to urge discipline and to correct the errors.
5. Timothy was sent by the apostle to assist in solving the problems in the church at Corinth (1 Corinthians 4:17).
6. There are four important topics discussed in this Epistle:
   a. Disorders in the church
   b. Gifts of the Holy Spirit
   c. Resurrection
   d. Matter of making collections

General Outline

I. GRAVITY OF REPORTS RECEIVED (1:1-6:20)
II. GUIDANCE TO RECTIFY AND REFORM (7:1-16:24)

Detailed Outline

I. GRAVITY OF REPORTS RECEIVED (1:1-6:20)
   A. Dedication (1:1-9)
      1. Consecrated Worker Called of God and a Colleague (1:1)
      2. Church Witnessing Called to Be Saints of the Lord (1:2)

3. Commendation of the Gift of Grace in Them (1:3-6)
4. Comforting Assurance in View of His Return (1:7-9)

B. Divisions (1:10–2:16)
1. Charge to the Saints at Corinth (1:10-12)
   a. Desire of Paul for Unity and Fellowship (1:10)
   b. Declaration regarding Contentions among Them (1:11)
   c. Dissension of Believers in Corinth (1:12)
2. Challenge (1:13-17)
   a. Person of Christ Alone Sufficient (1:13)
   b. Practice concerning Baptism (1:14-16)
   c. Preaching of the Cross of Christ (1:17)
3. Cross (1:18-25)
   a. Message of the Cross Contrasted (1:18)
   b. Method of Publication by Preaching (1:19-21)
   c. Manifestation of the Power of God (1:22-25)
      (1) Signs Sought by the Jews (1:22)
      (2) Stumblingblock and Stupidity to Unbelievers (1:23)
      (3) Strength and Salvation to All Who Believe (1:24-25)
4. Choice (1:26-31)
   a. Few among the Many Called of God (1:26)
   b. Foolish among the Wise of the World (1:27)
   c. Feeble among the Strong Called (1:27-28)
   d. Features Accorded to Those Called (1:29-31)
      (1) Wisdom
      (2) Righteousness
      (3) Sanctification
      (4) Redemption
5. Concern of the Apostle (2:1-5)
   a. Presentation of Christ to the Corinthians (2:1-2)
   b. Preaching of Christ in Weakness and Fear (2:3-4)
   c. Power of Christ Shown through His Spirit (2:4-5)
6. Cure of the Saints (2:6-16)
   a. Mystery of the Wisdom of God (2:6-8)
   b. Manifold Wonders of God Not by Human Wisdom (2:9)
   c. Ministry of the Word among the Saints (2:10-13)
      (1) Revelation of the Deep Things of God (2:10)

    c. Married Expected to Be:
       (1) Sincere with Each Other (7:10-11)
       (2) Secure with One Partner (7:12-14)
       (3) Sure with Fidelity and Faith (7:15-16)
  2. Movements of Believers (7:17-24)
    a. Called of God in Any Given Circumstance (7:17-19)
    b. Continuing according to the Will of God (7:20-22)
    c. Committing One's Self to God Where We Are (7:23-24)
    d. Caring about Right Relationships (7:25-28)
    e. Concentrating on the Important Things of Life (7:29-35)
    f. Conducting One's Self Faithfully before the Lord (7:36-40)
  3. Meats, Liberty, and Limitations (8:1-13)
    a. Appeal for Love in Matters of Eating Meats (8:1-3)
    b. Ability to Live in the Will of God (8:4-11)
       (1) Competence to Live for Christ in an Unbelieving World (8:4-6)
       (2) Consideration Lest Others Should Be Injured (8:7-8)
       (3) Controlling One's Own Liberty for His Sake (8:10-11)
    c. Abstinence for Love's Sake Where Needed (8:12-13)
B. 1 Corinthians 9
  1. Vocation of the Minister of Christ (9:1)
  2. Vindication of Ability in Service (9:2-6)
  3. Vineyard Activities of the Minister (9:7-18)
    a. Provision Made for the Worker (9:7)
    b. Planting Done by the Workers (9:7)
    c. Pastoral Care by the Worker (9:7)
    d. Partakers Together of the Work (9:8-13)
    e. Preaching and Responsibility in the Work (9:14-18)
  4. Vitality of the Minister (9:19-27)
    a. Identification according to Need (9:19-23)
    b. Intensity of Action to Gain a Prize (9:24-26)
    c. Internal Aspect of Self Discipline (9:27)
C. 1 Corinthians 10
  1. Warning Recorded by way of Illustration (10:1-15)

E. 1 Corinthians 12
    1. Endowment of the Gifts of the Holy Spirit (12:1-11)
        a. Spiritual and Distinctive (12:1-3)
        b. Serviceable and Directional (12:4-7)
        c. Several and Diverse in Kind (12:8-11)
        d. Sovereign Will of God (12:11)
    2. Example of Unity in the Body (12:12-27)
        a. Holiness of Each and Every Member of the Body (12:12-13)
        b. Harmony of Each Part in Relation to the Others (12:14-21)
        c. Honor of Each Part in Equality to Each Other (12:22-27)
    3. Exponents of the Gifts Given (12:28-31)
        a. Apostles and Others Mentioned in Order (12:28-29)
        b. Association of Different Gifts by One Spirit (12:30)
        c. Aspiration for the Best Gifts Urged (12:31)
F. 1 Corinthians 13
    1. Challenge of Love (13:1-3)
        a. Speak with Love (13:1)
        b. Understand with Love (13:2)
        c. Give with Love (13:3)
    2. Character of Love (13:4-8)
        a. Nine Negative Features
        b. Seven Positive Features
    3. Contrasts of Love (13:9-12)
        a. Ignorance Now—Knowledge Then (13:9,12)
        b. Imperfection Now—Perfection Then (13:10,12)
        c. Immaturity Now—Maturity Then (13:11-12)
        d. Importance Now—Love Over All (13:13)
G. 1 Corinthians 14
    1. Aim in the Ministry (14:1-6)
        a. Speak with Clarity (14:1-3)
        b. Speak with Comfort (14:3-4)
        c. Speak with Conviction (14:5-6)
    2. Ability to Be Definite and Decisive (14:7-11)
    3. Admonition to Understand (14:12-40)
        a. Concerning Speaking, Praying, and Singing (14:12-17)

2 Corinthians

Notes

1. This letter was probably written a few months after the first Epistle to the believers in Corinth and is evidently a reply to that letter.
2. Titus brought good news to Paul from the church at Corinth (2 Corinthians 7:6-7) which comforted the Apostle.
3. Titus probably also brought news of the Judaizing party who questioned Paul's motives and claims.
4. Paul replies to their charges in this Epistle (2 Corinthians 11:16-12:10).
5. Soon after writing the first Epistle, Paul was probably forced to flee for his life (2 Corinthians 1:8-11).
6. It has been observed that:
   a. 2 Corinthians 1:12-7:16 deals with the past
   b. 2 Corinthians 8:1-9:15 deals with the present
   c. 2 Corinthians 10:1-13:14 deals with the future

General Outline

I. VINDICATION OF THE MINISTRY (1:1-3:18)
II. VALIDITY OF THE MINISTRY (4:1-5:21)
III. VERIFICATION OF THE MINISTRY (6:1-10:18)
IV. VIEW OF THE MINISTER (11:1-13:14)

Detailed Outline

I. VINDICATION OF THE MINISTRY (1:1-3:18)
   A. Explanation (1:1-24)
      1. Cordiality of Greeting from Paul and Timothy (1:1-2)
      2. Comfort in Experiences Together (1:3-7)

   a. Sharing
   b. Serving
   c. Suffering
3. Calamities Endured for the Work's Sake (1:8-11)
   a. Trouble—Pressed out of Measure and in Despair (1:8)
   b. Trusting—Personally in the Lord for Deliverance (1:9-10)
   c. Thanksgiving and Prayer in Fellowship with Many (1:11)
4. Conviction and Testimony Confirmed (1:12-14)
   a. Motives—Simplicity and Sincerity of Conscience (1:12-14)
   b. Movements—Suggested by the Apostle (1:15-16)
   c. Meaning—Service with Conviction (1:17-24)
      (1) Honest
      (2) Heartwhole
B. Encouragement (2:1-17)
   1. Facts Stated by Paul (2:1-4)
      a. Lessons Learned from Previous Experience (2:1-2)
      b. Letter Loaded with Sorrow and Heart-searching (2:3-4)
      c. Love That Lightens Anxiety and Concern (2:4)
   2. Forgiveness in Love for the Penitent (2:5-11)
      a. Pain, yet Consolation for the Apostle (2:5)
      b. Punishment to Cease for the Penitent One (2:6-7)
      c. Proof of Loving Concern for the Penitent (2:8-11)
C. Exposition (3:1-18)
   1. Commendation Mutual between Them (3:1-4)
      a. Proof Evident in Paul's Own Character (3:1)
      b. Publicity Evident before All to Know (3:2)
      c. Place Enshrined in the Hearts of the Believers (3:3-4)
   2. Confirmation of God's Enabling (3:5-12)
      a. Competence to Serve by His All-sufficiency (3:5-6)
      b. Consequence of Spirit's Ministry—Glory (3:7-9)
      c. Conditions of the Law Surpassed by Christ (3:10-12)
   3. Contrast between Sinai and Christ (3:13-18)
      a. Greatness of the Law of Moses (3:13-15)

      b. Gravity of the Loss;Their Blindness (3:14-15)

      c. Glory of the Lord—Liberty in Christ Jesus (3:16-18)

II. VALIDITY OF THE MINISTRY (4:1–5:21)

    A. Expression (4:1-18)

      1. Truth regarding the Ministry (4:1-2)

        a. Reception of the Ministry and Mercy to Continue (4:1)

        b. Renouncement of Evil Behavior (4:2)

        c. Recognition of Commendable Behavior (4:2)

      2. Testimony of the Gospel (4:3-6)

        a. Their Ruin—Blindness to the Light in Unbelief (4:3-4)

        b. Their Redemption—Belief in That Light (4:5-6)

        c. The Radiance of the Shining Light of the Gospel (4:6)

      3. Treasure (4:7)

        a. Priceless Acquisition

        b. Pots Available

        c. Power Acknowledged

      4. Trouble That Assails the Servants (4:8-12)

        a. Perplexed but Not in Despair (4:8)

        b. Persecuted but Not Destroyed (4:9-10)

        c. Pursued by Death—That His Life be Made Manifest (4:11-12)

      5. Trust of Paul in the Lord (4:13-18)

        a. Reassurance Expressed by the Apostle in the Lord (4:13-14)

        b. Resurrection Expected:A Unifying Act (4:14)

        c. Renewal Experienced in Christ Each Day (4:15-16)

        d. Reward—"Eternal weight of glory" (4:17-18)

    B. Example (5:1-13)

      1. Circumstances of the Servant's Dwelling (5:1-5)

        a. Tent in Question Dissoluble (5:1)

        b. Tenant in Residence for a Limited Time (5:2-4)

        c. Teaching Intended for Comfort and Assurance (5:4-5)

      2. Confidence in God's Plan for One's Life (5:6-9)

        a. Promise of Home (5:6,8)

b. Practice of Holiness (5:7)
c. Pleasure to Him (5:9)
3. Concern of Every Believer (5:10-13)
a. Review of the Servant's Work (5:10)
b. Recognition of Urgency in the Work (5:11)
c. Rectitude of All Believers Required (5:12-13)
C. Evidences (5:14-21)
1. Relationship with Christ in Ministry (5:14-17)
a. New Concept—Love of Christ Constraining (5:14-15)
b. New Creature—Life of Christ Within (5:16-17)
c. New Control—Law of the Spirit of Life in Christ Now Operative (cf. Romans 8:2) (5:17)
2. Reconciliation by God of Sinners through Christ (5:18-19)
3. Representation of God by Believers in the World (5:20)
4. Righteousness of God for Us by Christ's Work (5:21)

III. VERIFICATION OF THE MINISTRY (6:1-10:18)
A. Exhortation (6:1-7:1)
1. Sincerity Shown in a Summary of Service (6:1-3)
a. No Wasted Provision of Grace in Service (6:1)
b. No Excuse—A Prophet's Pronouncement (cf. Isaiah 49:8) (6:2)
c. No Offence Proffered by the Lord's Servants (6:3)
d. No Blame Presented against the Ministry (6:3)
2. Suffering in the Service of Christ (6:4-10)
a. Endurance in Service As Ministers of Christ (6:4-5)
b. Example in Service As Enabled by the Holy Spirit (6:6-7)
c. Experience in Service: A Great Variety (6:8-9)
d. Enrichment in Service As Making Many Rich (6:10)
3. Separation of the Servant in His Service (6:11-7:1)
a. Concern of the Apostle for the Believers (6:11-13)
b. Contrasts of Believers and Unbelievers (6:14-16)
c. Communion of the Father with His Children (6:18)
d. Cleansing of Believers Incumbent on Us All (7:1)
B. Entreaty (7:2-16)
1. Courtesy of Paul to Corinthian Believers (7:2-3)

      a. No Cause to Refuse Fellowship with Him (7:2)

      b. No Corruption of Which to Repent in His Service (7:2)

      c. No Condemnation to Believers in Corinth (7:3)

  2. Conflict of the Apostle in Macedonia (7:5)

      a. Foes on Every Side Giving Him No Rest

      b. Fears Outside Giving Trouble and Burdens

      c. Fears Inside Giving No Assurance to the Flesh

  3. Comfort of God for His Servants (7:6-7)

      a. Cast Down by Pressures Around (7:6)

      b. Consoled by Believers and Titus (7:7)

      c. Contented by the Report Titus Brought (7:7)

  4. Confirmation of Their Mutual Fellowship (7:8-16)

      a. Regrets of the Apostle Turned to Satisfaction (7:8)

      b. Repentance of the Believers a Healthy Sign (7:9-10)

      c. Rejoicing of the Apostle for Them All (7:11-13)

      d. Result: Truth Tested and Triumphant (7:14-16)

C. Exercise (8:1–9:15)

  1. Collections for Needy Believers (8:1-7)

      a. In Affliction Even So the Believers Gave (8:1-2)

      b. In Affection Offering Gifts and Themselves (8:3-5)

      c. In Abundance Evidenced by Their Willing Gifts (8:4-7)

  2. Christ Jesus Ever An Example to Us All (8:8-9)

      a. Proving of Their Love a Result of His Love

      b. Price of Our Lives Paid by Him

      c. Poverty He Endured Brought Riches to Us

  3. Cooperation Together in His Service (8:10-15)

      a. Expediency in Being Ready to Continue (8:10-11)

      b. Equality in Bearing the Burdens Together (8:12-14)

      c. Enough in Being Sufficiently Provided For (8:15)

  4. Confidence in Fellowship between Them (8:16-24)

      a. In the Brethren Who Were Coming to Them (8:16-18)

      b. In the Believers Who Would Receive Them (8:19-22)

      c. In the Bond of Love Expressed among Them (8:23-24)

C. Career of Paul Recorded in Outline (11:16–12:6)
   1. Foolishness of the Flesh Conflicting with Service (11:16-21)
   2. Fatigue and Fears Continually to Be Faced (11:22-28)
   3. Fortitude and Faith Constantly in Evidence (11:29-33)
   4. Facts and Forbearance concerning Himself (12:1-6)
D. Commitment of Paul to the Lord's Will (12:7-11)
   1. Trust in Suffering Physically (12:7-8)
   2. Triumph in Sustaining the Thorn (12:9)
   3. Testimony of Strength out of Weakness (12:10-11)
E. Character of Paul Revealed (12:10-11)
   1. Patient Deeds He Wrought among Them (12:12)
   2. Persistent Daring of His Service (12:12-14)
   3. Purpose and Desire towards Them (12:14-18)
F. Coming of Paul to Visit Them (12:19-21)
   1. Warning of What Might Be Revealed (12:19-20)
   2. Waywardness of the Unrepentant (12:21)
G. Coming Visit of Paul Explained (13:1-6)
   1. Purpose
   2. Proof
   3. Power
H. Concern Paul Experienced (13:7-10)
   1. Truth
   2. Test
   3. Treatment
I. Conclusion of Paul's Epistle (13:11-14)
   1. Good Wishes
   2. Greetings
   3. Grace

GALATIANS

—◆—

NOTES

1. This letter was written to the churches in Galatia of which Pisidian Antioch, Iconium, and Lystra were a part.
2. The Galatian churches seemed to have lent a ready ear to the Judaizers who had followed Paul on his journeys.
3. These Judaizers demanded a scrupulous observation of the Mosaic law along with faith in Christ.
4. This Epistle is in answer to their teaching and activity.
5. Unlike other Epistles it has but one subject: the complete emancipation of believers in Christ from the law of Moses, except in so far as it was ratified by Christ.
6. There is a great deal of information about Paul's own career in this Epistle (Galatians 1:11-2:21).
7. This Epistle has been called the "Charter of Christian liberty."
8. The name of Christ is mentioned forty-three times.
9. The word "freedom" in one form or another is mentioned eleven times.
10. Note the references to the Holy Spirit (Galatians 3:2,3,5,14; 4:6,9; 5:16,17,18,22,25; 6:8).
11. Note the references to the cross of Christ (Galatians 1:4; 2:20; 3:1,13; 5:11,24; 6:12,14).
12. Note four downward steps:
    a. Removed from Christ (1:6)
    b. Bewitched by others (3:1-4)
    c. Fallen from grace (5:4)
    d. Hindered you (5:7)

GENERAL OUTLINE

I. JUSTIFICATION BY FAITH (1:1-3:5)
II. JUSTIFICATION AND FREEDOM (3:6-4:31)
III. JUSTIFICATION AND FIDELITY (5:1-6:18)

DETAILED OUTLINE

I. JUSTIFICATION BY FAITH (1:1–3:5)
   A. Galatians 1
      1. Definition of Apostleship Given (1:1)
         a. Paul—Not by Human Appointment
         b. Person of Christ and God the Father Called Him
         c. Power of the Resurrection a Guarantee to Him
      2. Description of Greetings and Grace to All (1:2-4)
         a. Company Who Sent Greetings in His Name (1:2-3)
         b. Complaint Dealt With—Our Sins (1:4)
         c. Consequence of His Death—Our Deliverance (1:4)
         d. Cause Declared—According to the Will of God (1:4)
      3. Directive to Glory and Praise (1:5)
      4. Departure and a Declaration (1:6–3:5)
         a. Removal from the Foundation of Faith in Christ (1:6-9)
            (1) Surprise (1:6)
            (2) Sadness (1:6)
            (3) Seducers (1:7)
            (4) Sentence (1:8-9)
         b. Reception of a Divine Message from the Lord (1:10-16)
            (1) Paul's Conviction (1:10)
            (2) Paul's Claim (1:11-12)
            (3) Paul's Conversion (1:13-16)
         c. Remembrances Recalled by Paul (1:16-20)
            (1) His Refusal to Consult with Men (1:16-17)
            (2) His Retreat into Arabia (1:17)
            (3) His Return to Jerusalem (1:18-20)
         d. Rejoicing among the Believers at Paul's Conversion (1:21-24)
   B. Galatians 2:1–3:5
      1. Reassurance Given Paul and His Co-workers (2:1-10)
         a. Communication with the Elders at Jerusalem (2:1-2)
         b. Conference with the Assembly There (2:3-8)
         c. Commendation to the Work of the Lord (2:9-10)
      2. Resistance of the Circumcision Party (2:11-14)
         a. Paul's Courage in Maintaining the Truth (2:11)

        b. Peter's Compromise with the Judaizers (2:12-13)

        c. Paul's Challenge to Them All and Peter (2:14)

    3. Redemptive Work of Christ Alone Contrasted to the Works of the Law (2:15-19)

    4. Righteousness of Christ—His Faith Within (2:20-21)

    5. Return to the Works of the Law Contrasted to the Complete Sufficiency of the Work of the Spirit (3:1-5)

II. JUSTIFICATION AND FREEDOM (3:6–4:31)

  A. Galatians 3:6–4:7

    1. Justification by Faith Illustrated in Abraham (3:6-9)

    2. Just "Shall live by faith" Contrasted to Works (3:10-12)

    3. Junction of Jew and Gentile in Christ by Faith (3:13-25)

        a. Argument relating to the Promise (3:13-18)

        b. Answer relating to the Provision Made (3:19-25)

    4. Justified Believers in a New Relationship (3:26–4:7)

        a. Adoption into the Family (3:26)

        b. Association of All One in Christ (3:27-29)

        c. Analogy of the Heir (4:1-3)

        d. Activity of Christ for Us (4:4-7)

  B. Galatians 4:8-31

    1. Lapse into Legality a Most Profitless Business (4:8-11)

    2. Labor and Love Discussed by Paul (4:12-19)

    3. Loyalty or Loss? "I stand in doubt of you" (4:20-21)

    4. Lessons on Liberty from Sarah and Hagar (4:22-31)

III. JUSTIFICATION AND FIDELITY (5–6)

  A. Galatians 5

    1. Application of the Allegory (5:1-15)

        a. Liberty in the Lord Alone (5:1-6)

        b. Leaven of the Law Brings Hindrances and Confusion (5:7-12)

        c. Licence and Lust—Love Triumphs over All (5:13-15)

    2. Activities in the Spirit (5:16-26)

        a. Faith in Exercise (5:16-25)

            (1) Walk In (5:16)

            (2) Led By (5:18)

            (3) Live In (5:25)

EPHESIANS

NOTES

1. Ephesus was the second largest city in the Roman Empire in Paul's day. Acts 20:31 tells us that he stayed there for three years.

2. The Apostle must have paid at least two visits to Ephesus as the following suggests (Acts 18:18-19; 19:1-22; 1 Timothy 1:3).

3. It would seem that there was an assembly of believers at Ephesus before Paul's first visit to them (Acts 18:24-19:2).

4. This Epistle was probably written during Paul's first imprisonment in Rome and was in the form of a circular.

5. The subject of the Epistle appears to be the church's vocation and unity within, and with Christ.

6. The term "heavenly places" occurs five times (Ephesians 1:3,20; 2:6; 3:10; 6:12).

7. The Holy Spirit is mentioned four times (Ephesians 1:13; 2:18; 3:16; 5:18).

8. The word "grace" occurs twelve times.

9. The word "riches" is mentioned five times (Ephesians 1:7,18; 2:7; 3:8,16).

10. In Ephesians we see the church as
    a. A body
    b. A building
    c. A bride

11. The believer is seen as
    a. Raised
    b. Seated
    c. Reigning with Christ

12. Christian character is referred to as
    a. Acting
    b. Walking
    c. Talking

13. Ephesus was the home of the great image Diana (Acts 19:27).

14. The ruins of Ephesus are now some twenty miles from the sea.

GENERAL OUTLINE

I.   AFFIRMATION OF DOCTRINE (1:1–3:21)
II. APPLICATION OF DEEDS (4:1–6:24)

DETAILED OUTLINE

I.   AFFIRMATION OF DOCTRINE (1:1–3:21)
    A. Ephesians 1
       1. Persons Involved in This Letter (1:1-2)
          a. Authority of the Apostle by the Will of God (1:1)
          b. Addressed, the Saints and Faithful Ones (1:1)
          c. Ascription of Grace and Peace to Them All (1:2)
       2. Purpose Revealed in Christ (1:3-4)
          a. Blessings to, and from God, to Them (1:3)
          b. Bounty of the Privileges in Christ (1:3)
          c. Blamelessness Enjoyed because of His Work (1:4)
       3. Praise of the Glory of His Grace (1:5-6)
          a. Predestination for the Chosen in Him (1:5)
          b. Adoption Ensured for His Children (1:5)
          c. Reception: Being Accepted in the Believed (1:6)
       4. Purchase and Possession (1:7)
          a. Redemption through His Blood Personal
          b. Remission of Sins—Forgiveness Real
          c. Riches of His Grace Demonstrated
       5. Process Outlined (1:8-14)
          a. Pleasure Shown in Making Known His Will to Us (1:8-9)
          b. Program Set Out (1:10)
             (1) In One
             (2) In Christ
             (3) In Him
          c. Possession Secured according to His Purpose (1:11)
          d. Purpose Signifying Our High Calling in Christ (1:12)
          e. Partakers Sealed with the Holy Spirit of Promise (1:13)
          f. Pledge Satisfactory (1:14)

6. Prayer of the Apostle (1:15-23)
   a. Contentment in the Knowledge of Their Faith (1:15)
   b. Continuity in Thanksgiving and Prayer for Them (1:16)
   c. Care of the Apostle Shown for Them in His Intercession (1:17-19)
      (1) That He May Give Wisdom (1:17)
      (2) That He May Give Revelation (1:17)
      (3) That He May Give Knowledge (1:17)
      (2) That He May Give Enlightenment (1:18)
      (3) That He May Give the Greatness of His Power (1:19)
   d. Christ Revealed to Them in (1:20-23)
      (1) His Resurrection (1:20)
      (2) His Glorification (1:20)
      (3) His Elevation (1:21-22)
      (4) His Association (1:22-23)

B. Ephesians 2
   1. Mankind before God (2:1-3)
      a. Condition—Dead in Trespasses and Sins (2:1)
      b. Character—Desire for the Flesh and the World (2:2)
      c. Consequence—Depraved and Destined for Judgement (2:3)
   2. Method of God to Redeem (2:4-10)
      a. Ruined Sinners—Object of His Mercy and Love (2:4-5)
      b. Redeemed—Quickened Together with Christ (2:5)
      c. Resurrection—Raised Up to Sit Together with Him (2:6)
      d. Riches—His Grace yet to Be Revealed through Christ (2:7-9)
      e. Responsibility—To Fulfill His Purposes for Us (2:10)
   3. Manner in Which God Redeems (2:11-22)
      a. Past Remembered (2:11-13)
         (1) Helpless Condition of the Gentiles (2:11)
         (2) Hostility to the Commonwealth of Israel (2:12)
         (3) Happy Condition—Brought Nigh to God (2:13)
      b. Present Reviewed (2:14-22)
         (1) Success and Scope of Christ's Work for Us (2:14-17)
         (2) Satisfaction Resulting from His Work (2:18)

(3) Significance of His Work for All Believers (2:19-22)
(a) Unity in Christ for All Believers
(b) Uniqueness of the Building Unified
(c) Understanding Their Position

C. Ephesians 3
1. Mystery Now Revealed (3:1-12)
   a. Declaration by the Apostle (3:1-5)
   b. Design of God Declared for Jew and Gentile (3:6)
   c. Dedication of the Servant Revealed (3:7-9)
      (1) Unmerited Recognition by the Lord (3:7-8)
      (2) Unworthy Recipient of Grace and Gift (3:8)
      (3) Unsearchable Riches and Fellowship (3:8-9)
   d. Display of Hidden Things (3:11-13)
      (1) Object—Wisdom of God Revealed to the Church (3:10)
      (2) Origin—Eternal Purposes in Christ Jesus (3:11)
      (3) Obligation on Us All—Access with Boldness (3:12)
2. Means at Our Disposal—Prayer (3:13-21)
   a. Desire—That They Should Not Faint at His Troubles (3:13)
   b. Devotion—The Ministry of Intercession by Paul (3:14-15)
   c. Dwelling of Christ Within—Rooted and Grounded in Love (3:16-17)
   d. Discernment—Comprehension of the Love of God (3:18-19)
   e. Doxology—"Unto him that is able...unto him be glory" (3:20-21)

II. APPLICATION OF DEEDS (4:1–6:24)
A. Ephesians 4
1. Walk Worthy of the Vocation (4:1-16)
   a. Unity of the Spirit Expressed in the Walk (4:1-3)
   b. Uniqueness Demonstrated Sevenfold (4:4-6)
   c. Usefulness Intended for Everyone (4:7-11)
      (1) Selection and Gift (4:7)
      (2) Supremacy of Christ (4:10)
      (3) Sovereignty (4:11)

    d. Understanding Necessary of the Gifts and Their Purpose (4:12–16)
      (1) Purpose of the Gifts Shown (4:12-13)
        (a) Maturity of the Saints (4:12)
        (b) Ministry to Their Edification (4:12)
        (c) Measuring up to the Stature of Christ (4:13)
      (2) Perception as a Result (4:14-16)
        (a) No More Infancy
        (b) No More Ignorance
        (c) No More Instability
      (3) Progress in Speaking the Truth in Love—Strength Supplied to Every Part (4:15-16)
  2. Walk Not in Vanity (4:17-32)
    a. Sinful Practices of the Past at an End (4:17-19)
    b. Separation from Those Practices a Fact (4:20-22)
    c. Sanctification Now to Be in Evidence (4:23-24)
    d. Sincerity the Hallmark of Our Actions (4:25-27)
    e. Service to Others (4:28-32)
      (1) Work with the Hands
      (2) Witness by the Mouth
      (3) Wholesomeness in Attitude
B. Ephesians 5
  1. Walk in Love (cf. Revelation 2:4) (5:1-7)
    a. Reason—To Follow an Example (5:1-2)
    b. Refusal—To Return to Old Ways of Sin (5:3-4)
    c. Rejectors of Truth—Have No Inheritance in Christ (5:5)
    d. Reassurance—A Word of Exhortation and Comfort (5:6-7)
  2. Walk in Light (5:8-14)
    a. Aware of the Position in Which We Were and Now Are (5:8-9)
    b. A Work of Proving Positively and Negatively in Our Walk (5:10-12)
    c. Awake to the Many Perils Surrounding Believers (5:13-14)
  3. Walk Carefully or Circumspectly (5:15-33)
    a. Manner of Walking in Wisdom—Understanding the Will of God (5:15-17)

     b. Means—Being Filled with the Holy Spirit (5:18)
     c. Manifestation of Wisdom in (5:19-21)
        (1) Speaking
        (2) Singing
        (3) Submitting to One Another
     d. Marriage Illustrating (5:22-23)
        (1) Pattern of Submission and Love (5:22-25)
        (2) Preparation of the Bride (5:26)
        (3) Presentation of the Bride (5:27)
        (4) Progress of Love—Care and Identity (5:28-31)
        (5) Plainness of Speech—Church and Bride
            (5:32-33)
C. Ephesians 6
    1. Witness At Home (6:1-9)
     a. Children to Parents—Obey and Honor (6:1-3)
     b. Fathers to Children—Help, Not Provocation (6:4)
     c. Servants to Masters—Obey as the Lord (6:5-8)
     d. Masters to Servants—Care, Not Threatening (6:9)
    2. Warfare in the World (6:10-22)
     a. Power Available to Strengthen in Witness (6:10)
     b. Provision Made for All Believers by the Lord
        (6:11-13)
     c. Preparation for the Task (6:14-17)
        (1) Girdle
        (2) Breastplate
        (3) Shoes
        (4) Shield
        (5) Helmet
        (6) Sword
     d. Prayerful Supplication in Sincerity for the Apostle
        (6:18-19)
     e. Personal Confidences Given (6:20-22)
     f. Parting and Benediction for the Believers at
        Ephesus (6:23-24)
        (1) Peace
        (2) Love
        (3) Faith
        (4) Grace

Philippians

Notes

1. This Epistle was one of the prison Epistles and was written from Rome probably about A.D. 63.
2. Paul first visited Philippi on his second missionary journey with Silas (Acts 16:9-13).
3. He again visited the city on his third missionary journey about A.D. 57-58 (Acts 20:1-6).
4. Philippi is better known today as the first city in Europe to receive the gospel rather than the place where Octavius defeated Brutus and thus ended the Roman Republic.
5. Epaphroditus had been sent from the believers in Philippi with a gift to the Apostle during his imprisonment in Rome (Philippians 2:25; 4:18).
6. This letter is the Apostle's acknowledgment of the gift with his thanks for their fellowship.
7. The words "joy", "rejoice", etc. occur about eighteen times.

General Outline

- I.   REJOICING IN SUFFERING (1:1-30)
- II. REJOICING IN SERVICE (2:1-30)
- III. REJOICING IN SECURITY (3:1-21)
- IV. REJOICING IN THE SAVIOR (4:1-23)

Detailed Outline

- I. REJOICING IN SUFFERING (1:1-30)
  - A. Thankfulness of Paul (1:1-7)
    1. Remembrance in Prayer of Fellowship Together (1:1-3)
    2. Requests in Prayer with Joy for Them All (1:4)

      3. Reassurance in Partnership Together in the Gospel (1:5-7)
         a. Continuity
         b. Confidence
         c. Coming Day of Christ
  B. Triumph in the Lord (1:8-18)
      1. In Prayer for Them All in Love (1:8-11)
      2. In the Palace for All to Hear and Know (1:12-14)
      3. In Preaching for a Variety of Reasons (1:15-18)
  C. Truth of God Set Forth (1:19-21)
      1. Hope of Continuing to Honor the Lord Expressed (1:19-21)
      2. Hesitation of Mind—To Go or Stay? (1:22-24)
      3. Help of the Apostle Still Available (1:25-26)
      4. Holiness of Fellowship among Believers (1:27)
      5. Harness of Fellowship with Christ in Service (1:28-30)

II. REJOICING IN SERVICE (2:1-30)
  A. Exhortation from the Prison-bound Apostle (2:1-4)
      1. Fellowship of the Holy Spirit in Christ (2:1)
      2. Fulfillment of Joy in Being Like-Minded (2:2)
      3. Faithfulness of Each with the Other in Him (2:3-4)
  B. Explanation Found in Christ Himself (2:5-11)
      1. Incarnation of Christ (2:5-7)
      2. Humiliation of Christ (2:8)
      3. Exaltation of Christ (2:9-11)
         a. Every Name (2:9)
         b. Every Knee (2:10)
         c. Every Tongue (2:11)
  C. Expression of His Life within Us (2:12-16)
      1. Working Out What He Has Put within Us (2:12)
      2. Working within to Do His Good Pleasure (2:13)
      3. Without Dispute Expressing His Will and Purpose (2:14)
      4. Witness of the Word in a Christ-Rejecting World (2:15-16)
  D. Example of the Apostle and His Co-workers (2:17-30)
      1. Paul—Who Knew What Sacrifice Really Meant (2:17-18)
      2. Timothy—Who Cared As Few Others Did (2:19-23)
      3. Epaphroditus—Who Was Like-Minded with Them All (2:25-30)

III. Rejoicing in Security (3:1-21)
    A. Looking Around—Beware of Legalists (3:1-3)
        1. Beware of Evil People (3:1-3)
        2. Beware of Evil Practices (3:1-2)
        3. Be Aware of the Privileges We Have in Christ (3:3)
    B. Looking Backward—Beguiled by the Law (3:4-9)
        1. Acknowledged Facts of Paul's Past Life (3:4-5)
        2. Activities Featuring His Past Way of Life (3:6)
        3. Ambition Formulated for Future Action (3:7-9)
            a. His Reckoning
            b. His Reasoning
            c. His Reception
            d. His Righteousness
    C. Looking Upward—Beholding the Lord (3:10-14)
        1. Power and Fellowship in Identity with the Lord (3:10)
        2. Pilgrim Following—Pressing toward the Mark (3:11-13)
        3. Pressing Forward and Ever Upward for the Prize (3:14)
    D. Looking Inside—Behavior in Living (3:15-21)
        1. Attainment in Faith and Unity of Mind (3:15-16)
        2. Attitude of Indifference and Distress (3:17-19)
        3. Anticipation in the Interest Focused on His Coming (3:20-21)

IV. REJOICING IN THE SAVIOR (4:1-23)
    A. Satisfaction in Joy among Believers (4:1-4)
        1. Standing Together Steadfast in the Lord (4:1)
        2. Synchronizing Thoughts in Oneness of Mind (4:2)
        3. Serving Together in Joy and Unity in Him (4:3-4)
    B. Secret of Joy in View of His Coming (4:5-7)
        1. Believer's Privilege in Prayer and Supplication (4:5-6)
        2. Believer's Prerogative in Praise and Thanksgiving (4:6)
        3. Believer's Position in Peace and Security in Christ (4:7)
    C. Scope of Joy in Experience (4:8-9)
        1. By Observation—"Whatsoever things" (4:8)
        2. By Examination—"If there be...think" (4:8)
        3. By Operation—"Learned...received...heard...seen...do" (4:9)
    D. Sufficiency of Joy in Christian Experience (4:10-23)
        1. Appreciation of Their Care by the Apostle (4:10)
        2. Acknowledged Contentment in Christ's Sufficiency (4:11-19)
        3. Apostolic Conclusion—Greeting with Grace (4:20-23)

COLOSSIANS

NOTES

1. Colossae was a large town in Asia Minor and like Laodicea was famous for its wool (Colossians 4:16).
2. It is doubtful whether Paul ever visited Colossae (Colossians 2:1).
3. Epaphras probably brought news of false doctrine at Colosse to Paul while in prison at Rome (Colossians 1:7; 4:12).
4. It appears that while Epaphras was in Rome he was also imprisoned with Paul (Philemon 23).
5. Tychicus probably carried this prison Epistle to the believers at Colossae along with that to Ephesus (Ephesians 6:21-22).
6. Onesimus probably went with him carrying a letter from Paul to Philemon (Philemon 12).
7. The false doctrine which Paul sought to deal with was twofold:
    a. Philosophical—claimed that God was too holy to make contact with flesh and remain undefiled, seeing that everything material was evil
    b. Ascetical—claimed that complete observance of the Mosaic law was essential to salvation
8. Both these ideas obviously challenged the preeminence of Christ (Colossians 1:18).
9. The words "Christ is all, and in all" (Colossians 3:11), may well crystallize the contents of the Epistle.

GENERAL OUTLINE

I.   SUPREMACY OF CHRIST (1:1-29)
II. SUFFICIENCY OF CHRIST (2:1-23)
III. SERVICE IN CHRIST (3:1-4:18)

DETAILED OUTLINE

I.   SUPREMACY OF CHRIST (1:1-29)
     A. Encouragement (1:1-8)
        1. Greetings from Paul and Timothy (1:1-2)

B. The Way (2:4-8)
  1. Danger of Beguiling Talk That Entices Away (2:4)
  2. Devotion to Behold in Their Order and Faith (2:5-7)
  3. Deceivers to Beware and Avoid along the Way (2:8)
C. The Work (2:9-15)
  1. Completeness of Christ Needs No Additions (2:9-10)
  2. Competence of Christ All Sufficient (2:11-13)
  3. Conclusion of Christ's Work Needs No Revision (2:14-15)
D. The Warning (2:16-23)
  1. Against Arguments—No Compromise with Conscience (2:16-17)
  2. Against Angel Worship—No Compromise in True Worship (2:18-19)
  3. Against Asceticism—No Compromise of Liberty in Christ (2:20-23)

III. SERVICE IN CHRIST (3:1-4:18)
  A. Fellowship (3:1-4)
    1. Attention for Heavenly Things with Risen Lord (3:1)
    2. Affection for Spiritual Things with Heaven in View (3:2-3)
    3. Appearance for Believers with Him in Glory (3:4)
  B. Fidelity (3:5-9)
    1. Purity in Living—Concerning Our Walk (3:5,7)
    2. Perils in Licence—Concerning God's Wrath (3:5-6)
    3. Purity of Lips—Concerning Our Words (3:8-9)
  C. Fruitfulness (3:10-17)
    1. Supply (3:10-11)
      a. Reclothed—"Put off"
      b. Renewed—"Put on"
    2. Signs Resulting (3:12-14)
    3. Service—Rule of Life Displayed (3:15-17)
  D. Family (3:18-4:1)
    1. Relationships (3:18-25)
      a. Wives
      b. Husbands
      c. Children
      d. Servants

1 THESSALONIANS

NOTES

1. Thessalonica is now the modern city of Salonica.
2. Paul first visited this city on his second missionary journey in company with Silas. He sought to do so again once or twice (1 Thessalonians 2:18).
3. It appears he was unable to visit the city again and sent Timothy in his place (1 Thessalonians 3:1-2).
4. 1 Thessalonians is probably Paul's first Epistle written and sent from Corinth about A.D. 52-54.
5. Timothy brought news to Paul of the Thessalonians' faith, love, and remembrances which was a comfort to Paul (1 Thessalonians 3:6-7).
6. It was at Thessalonica that Paul and his companions were referred to as, "These that have turned the world upside down" (Acts 17:6). This was no small compliment to their witness.
7. Both Epistles have much to say about the second coming of the Lord Jesus Christ.
8. 1 Thessalonians appears to have been written to answer:
    a. Criticism of Paul's motives (2:1-12)
    b. Certain vices among some of the believers (4:1-8; 5:1-11)
    c. Uneasiness about the fate of believers who had passed on (4:13-18)

GENERAL OUTLINE

   I.   SATISFACTION IN SERVICE (1:1–2:11)
  II.   SEQUEL IN SANCTIFICATION (2:12–4:12)
III.   SECOND COMING FOR THE SAINTS (4:13–5:28)

DETAILED OUTLINE

   I.   SATISFACTION IN SERVICE (1:1–2:11)
      A. 1 Thessalonians 1:1-10

      1. Grace of God and Peace to Them All (1:1)
      2. Gratitude of Paul to God for Them All (1:2-4)
         a. Prayer Continually Made for Them (1:2)
         b. Practice of Loving Labor in Faith (1:3)
         c. Patience of Hope in Christ (1:3)
         d. Position of Permanency in Christ (2:4)
      3. Gospel—All-Important Message from God (1:5-10)
         a. Demonstration of Power of the Gospel (1:5)
         b. Definite Evidence That Followed (1:6)
         c. Declared Example and Witness Effective (1:7-8)
         d. Decision Made (1:9)
         e. Dedication Made (1:9)
         f. Devotion to a Person (1:10)
         g. Deliverance Accomplished (1:10)
   B. 1 Thessalonians 2:1-11
      1. Six Negative Facts Referred to in Paul's Service (2:1-9)
         a. Not in Vain that He Came among Them (2:1)
         b. Not in Deceit, Guile, nor Uncleanness (2:3)
         c. Not with a Desire to Please Men (2:4)
         d. Not with Flattery or Covetousness (2:5)
         e. Not to Seek Personal Glory or Esteem (2:6)
         f. Not to Be a Burden to Them (2:9)
      2. Six Positive Facts in Paul's Service (2:2-11)
         a. Was Bold in the Face of Opposition (2:2)
         b. Was Gentle As a Mother with Her Child (2:7)
         c. Was Sincere in His Affection for Them (2:8)
         d. Was Honest in His Labors among Them (2:9)
         e. Was Exemplary in His Behavior among Them (2:10)
         f. Was Fatherly in His Comfort and Exhortation (2:11)

II. SEQUEL IN SANCTIFICATION (2:12–4:12)
   A. 1 Thessalonians 2:12-20
      1. Heard and Received the Word of Truth As from God (2:12-13)
      2. Harnessed Together and Resolute to Serve and Suffer in the Service of Christ (2:14-16)
      3. Hindrances Recognized As from Satan (2:17-18)

    4. Heart Rejoicing in Their Fellowship Together in the Prospect of the Return of Christ (2:19-20)

B. 1 Thessalonians 3:1–4:12

    1. Object of the Messenger Being Sent to Them (3:1-5)

        a. Establish the Believers in the Faith (3:1-2)

        b. Encourage Them to Endure Afflictions (3:3-4)

        c. Enquire of Their Spiritual State in Christ (3:5)

    2. Outlook of the Message Timothy Brought (3:6-7)

        a. Character of the Believers (3:6)

            (1) Faith

            (2) Love

            (3) Desire

        b. Comfort for the Apostle in Their Faithfulness (3:7)

        c. Consolation in Labor Well Spent on Them (3:7)

    3. Obligation of the Ministry on the Apostle (3:8-13)

        a. Appreciation of All God's Mercies to Them (3:8-11)

        b. Affection Abounding between Them in Christ (3:12)

        c. Anticipation of the Coming of Christ (3:13)

    4. Opportunity for the Minister in Service (4:1-4)

        a. Knowing Who to Please in Our Walk (4:1)

        b. Knowing What the Commandments Are (4:2)

        c. Knowing How to Live a Sanctified Life (4:3-4)

    5. Orderliness to be Manifested in Service (4:3-12)

        a. What to Avoid (4:3,5-6)

            (1) Fornication

            (2) Lust

            (3) Fraud

        b. What to Acquire (4:7-10)

            (1) A Holy Way of Life

            (2) A Holy Way of Love

        c. How to Act (4:11-12)

            (1) Studiously

            (2) Honestly

            (3) Diligently

III. SECOND COMING FOR THE SAINTS (4:13-5:28)

A. 1 Thessalonians 4:13-5:3

    1. Concerning the Saints Both Alive and Dead (4:13-15)

2 Thessalonians

Notes

1. Paul wrote the second Epistle to the Thessalonians to answer a misunderstanding about the return of Christ for and with His own (2 Thessalonians 2:1-12).
2. Paul also addressed the growing persecution and trouble from false teachers who had circulated a spurious letter as from Paul (2 Thessalonians 2:2).

General Outline

I. DECLARATION (1:1-12)
II. DISTINCTION (2:1-17)
III. DEMONSTRATION (3:1-18)

Detailed Outline

I. DECLARATION (1:1-12)
  A. Salutation from Paul, Silas, and Timothy (1:1-4)
    1. Greetings to Those in Fellowship with the Father (1:1-2)
    2. Growth in Faith, Love, and Fellowship Together (1:3)
    3. Glory in Faith, Patience, and Afflictions Endured (1:4)
  B. Suffering of the Saints (1:5-7)
    1. Righteousness of God in Permitting Suffering (1:5)
    2. Recompense to Those Who Trouble the Saints (1:6)
    3. Rest for the Saints with Christ at His Coming (1:7)
  C. Sentence Passed by God on the Wicked (1:8-10)
    1. Retribution on the Christ-Rejectors (1:8)
    2. Refusal to Honor the Son of God (1:8)
    3. Ruin Complete and Final (1:9-10)

1 TIMOTHY

NOTES

1. Timothy was probably a native of Lystra, the son of a Greek father and Jewish mother.
2. The name *Timothy* means "honored by God".
3. He was associated for some years with Paul in his missionary activities.
4. Timothy is mentioned with Paul in greetings sent to the churches in 2 Corinthians, Philippians, Colossians, and 1 and 2 Thessalonians and to Philemon.
5. Tradition says he was martyred at Ephesus.
6. The first Epistle was probably written about A.D. 64-66.
7. It appears to have been written to warn Timothy of heresies and to advise him on church order and conduct.
8. Note the words "a faithful saying" in 1:15 and 4:9.
9. 1 and 2 Timothy and Titus are known as the pastoral Epistles.

GENERAL OUTLINE

I. PURPOSE IN WRITING (1:1-17)
II. PERSONAL RESPONSIBILITY (1:18-3:16)
III. PRACTICE OF RIGHTEOUSNESS (4:1-6:21)

DETAILED OUTLINE

I. PURPOSE IN WRITING (1:1-17)
   A. Commencement of the Letter (1:1-2)
      1. The Apostle
      2. His Appointment
      3. His Association
   B. Caution Called For (1:3-4)
      1. Doctrines Being Taught Contrary to Truth (1:3)

2. Discussions on Unprofitable Questions (1:4)
3. Doing Deeds That Edify in the Faith (1:4)

C. Corrections Needed (1:5-10)
1. Purity in Devotion, Love, and Faith (1:5)
2. Pride in Designs Leads to Losing the Way (1:6-7)
3. Purpose in Desire for the Law Good (1:8-10)

D. Confession of the Apostle (1:11-16)
1. Privilege in Gospel Service (1:11)
2. Position Given to Paul in the Ministry (1:12)
3. Persecutor Though He Was in Ignorance (1:13)
4. Pardoned Sinner through Mercy and Grace (1:13-14)
5. Pattern for Those Who Follow After (1:15-16)
6. Praise and Benediction of Paul (1:17)

II. PERSONAL RESPONSIBILITY (1:18-3:16)
A. Plea to Timothy to Be Faithful in Service (1:18-20)
1. Fight from Which There Is No Discharge (1:18)
2. Faith a Sure Anchorage in the Fight (1:19)
3. Failure of Some Who Have Turned Aside (1:20)

B. Prayer and Exhortation (2:1-8)
1. What to Pray For (2:1-2)
a. All Men
b. All Kings
c. All Rulers
2. Why They Should Pray—It Is the Will of God (2:3-7)
3. Who Should Pray—All Men Everywhere (2:8)

C. Practice of Women in the Assembly (2:9-15)
1. In Their Dress as a Witness to Others (2:9)
2. In Their Duty in Witness and Work before Others (2:10-12)
3. In Their Deliverance in Times of Difficulty (2:13-15)

D. Pattern for the Servants of God (3:1-3)
1. Call and Desire to Work (3:1)
2. Character of the Work Not a Sinecure (3:2-7)
3. Competence for the Work (3:2,6,9,11)
4. Cooperation in the Work by the Wives (3:11)

E. Personally from Paul (3:14-16)
1. Motive in Writing before His Coming to Timothy (3:14-15)
2. Mystery of Godliness—The Incarnation of Christ (3:16)

    3. Manifesto of Faith to Timothy (3:16)
        a. Justification
        b. Identification
        c. Proclamation
        d. Glorification

III. PRACTICE OF RIGHTEOUSNESS (4:1–6:21)
    A. Warning against Apostates (4:1-3)
        1. Departure from the Faith—A Sign of the Latter Times (4:1)
        2. Deluded by Evil Spirits Who Deceive at Will (4:1)
        3. Doctrines from the Devil Himself (4:1)
        4. Deeds Contrary to the Scriptures (4:2-3)
    B. Watchfulness Necessary (4:4-8)
        1. Food Provided by God Worthy of Thanksgiving (4:4-5)
        2. Faith of Christ Contrasted to Fables (4:6-7)
        3. Fitness for the Lord's Work—Spiritual and Physical (4:8)
    C. Walk among Many Witnesses (4:9-16)
        1. Toiling and Trusting in the Lord's Work (4:9-10)
        2. Task by Example—Reading and Teaching (4:11-13)
        3. Testimony in the Work Resulting by Exercise (4:14-16)
            a. Caring for the Gift
            b. Concentrating on the Gift
            c. Continuing with the Gift
    D. Workers Together (5:1-14)
        1. Wisdom In Dealing with One Another in the Lord (5:1-2)
        2. Widows in the Church Gathering (5:3-16)
            a. Relations and Their Responsibilities (5:4,8)
            b. Relief to Widows in Real Need (5:4-16)
            c. Reports on Widows to Be Considered (5:5,9-10)
            d. Risks Possible with Some Younger Ones (5:6,11-13)
            e. Responsibility of the Younger Widows (5:14)
    E. Witness in the Assembly (5:17–6:21)
        1. Respect for Worthy Elders and Leaders (5:17)
        2. Rewards for Worthy Laborers (5:18)
        3. Rebuke Only for Proven Misbehavior (5:19-20)
        4. Request in the Charge (5:21-23)

2 TIMOTHY

NOTES

1. The second Epistle to Timothy was probably written about A.D. 67-68. This would have been at the close of Nero's reign and during Paul's second imprisonment.
2. Note the following indicated in this Epistle:
    a. Paul knew his end was near (4:6-8)
    b. He was probably suffering much discomfort (4:13)
    c. Many in Asia had repudiated him (1:15)
    d. Fellow laborers had gone on various errands (4:10-12)
    e. Paul longed for the company of two young men—Timothy and John Mark (4:9-11)

GENERAL OUTLINE

I.   TRUST OF SERVANTS (1:1-18)
II. TASKS OF SERVANTS (2:1-26)
III. TRUTH IN SERVICE (3:1-17)
IV. TRIALS OF SERVANTS (4:1-22)

DETAILED OUTLINE

I. TRUST OF SERVANTS (1:1-18)
    A. Greeting of Paul to Timothy (1:1-2)
        1. Privilege of Apostleship by the Will of God (1:1)
        2. Promise of Life in the Lord Jesus (1:1)
        3. Parental Care of the Apostle for Timothy (1:2)
    B. Gratitude (1:3-5)
        1. Paul's Conscience Satisfied regarding Intercession (1:3)
        2. Paul's Concern to See Timothy Again (1:4)
        3. Paul's Conviction regarding Timothy's Sincerity and Faith (1:5)

C. Gift (1:6-7)
   1. Reminding Timothy of the Gift He Received (1:6)
   2. Rekindling the Gift in Useful Service (1:6)
   3. Reasoning about the Gift (1:7)
      a. Power
      b. Love
      c. A Sound Mind
D. Gospel (1:8-12)
   1. Fellowship of the Gospel (1:8)
      a. Prisoner
      b. Partaker
   2. Features of the Gospel
      a. Glorious Savior
      b. Great Salvation
      c. Gratifying Sequel
   3. Fidelity to the Gospel (1:11-12)
      a. Appointment
      b. Assurance
      c. Ability
E. Guardianship (1:13-18)
   1. Aim to Hold Fast That Good Thing (1:13-14)
   2. Alternative to Turning Away from the Truth (1:15)
   3. Acknowledgement to Onesiphorus for Loving Service (1:16-18)

II. TASKS OF SERVANTS (2:1-26)
   A. Concentration in the Task (2:1-6)
      1. Lessons Learned to Be Handed on to Others (2:1-2)
      2. Life's Labors (2:3-6)
         a. Endure Rigors
         b. Endeavor Resourcefully
         c. Earn a Reward
   B. Consideration of the Task (2:7-13)
      1. Cause for Reflection—Remembering Essentials (2:7-8)
      2. Conflict to Remember—Recurring in Service (2:9-10)
      3. Conclusions Recorded—Repetition of "if" (2:11-13)
   C. Charge about the Task (2:14-18)
      1. Risk of Strife Offset by the Word of Truth (2:14)
      2. Resource in Study of the Word of God (2:15)
      3. Ruin in Subversion of the Truth (2:16-18)

D. Church and the Task (2:19-21)
   1. Foundation Unassailable—Standing Sure (2:19)
   2. Failures are Unusable in spite of Appearances (2:20)
   3. Fidelity is Unmistakable in Honorable Service (2:20-21)
E. Conduct in the Task (2:22-26)
   1. Attention to Testimony and Purity in Practice (2:22)
   2. Avoiding the Traps in Side Issues (2:23)
   3. Aptitude for Teaching and Patience in Instruction (2:24-25)
   4. Acknowledging Truth and Awareness of Snares (2:25-26)

III. TRUTH IN SERVICE (3:1-17)
A. Hard Times (3:1-5)
   1. Grievous Trials Arrive in the Latter Days (3:1-2)
      a. Depravity in Affection
      b. Disobedience to Authority
   2. Godless Traitors Appear (3:3-4)
      a. Lovers of Self
      b. Lovers of Pleasure
   3. Godly People Turn Away from Them Because (3:5)
      a. They Have No Faith
      b. They Have No Fruit
      c. They Have No Fellowship
B. Hostility to Truth (3:6-9)
   1. Evil Leaders Misleading the Uninformed (3:6)
   2. Ever Learning without Profit to Themselves (3:7)
   3. Ending in Loss as Those Here Named (3:8-8)
C. Honor to Teachers (3:10-13)
   1. Purpose in Manner of Life—Successfully Serving (3:10)
   2. Present Manner of Life for Paul—Suffering in Service (3:11-12)
   3. Perversion by Men of Lust Deceiving and Being Deceived (3:13)
D. Help from Teaching (3:14-17)
   1. Spiritual Food (3:14-15)
   2. Salient Features (3:16)
      a. Inspiration
      b. Instruction
   3. Satisfactorily Furnished by the Word of God (3:17)

IV. TRIALS OF SERVANTS (4:1-22)
  A. Command (4:1-2)
    1. Charge Given to Timothy in view of Christ's Coming (4:1)
    2. Continuity in Service to Rebuke, Reprove, and Exhort (4:2)
  B. Contrast (4:3-4)
    1. Dividing Factors Evident in the Latter Days (4:3)
    2. Doubtful Fancies Expressed in New Ideas (4:3)
    3. Desiring Fables Rather Than Truth (4:4)
  C. Concern (4:5)
    1. Endure the Rigors of Christian Service
    2. Evangelize Faithfully and Continuously
    3. Exercise the Gift Received
  D. Confidence (4:6-8)
    1. Paul's Submission to the Will of God (4:6)
    2. Paul's Service Outlined to Timothy (4:7)
      a. He Had Fought
      b. He Had Run
      c. He Had Kept the Faith
    3. Paul's Serenity in Knowing the Crown Awaited Him (4:8)
  E. Call (4:9-13)
    1. Circumstances—Departure and Devotion (4:9-11)
    2. Companions Desired—Timothy and Mark (4:11)
    3. Comforts Desired—Cloak, Books, and Parchments (4:13)
  F. Conclusion (4:14-22)
    1. Adversary and Victory (4:14-16)
    2. Assurance and Valediction (4:17-22)

TITUS

NOTES

1. All we know of Titus is gathered from Paul's writings.
2. Titus is not mentioned in the book of the Acts.
3. From the letter to the Galatians we learn the he was a Greek (Galatians 2:3).
4. He was associated with Paul in the work and went to Jerusalem with him and Barnabas (Galatians 2:1).
5. Paul must have had confidence in him seeing Titus went to Corinth on his behalf (2 Corinthians 8:6; 12:18).
6. He was also left in Crete by Paul to do important work among the churches there (Titus 1:5,9-14).
7. It has been said that this Epistle is a "priceless manual on pastoral advice."
8. Tradition says that after working in Dalmatia, Titus returned to Crete and worked there until his death at the age of ninety-four years.

GENERAL OUTLINE

   I. APPOINTMENTS (1:1-16)
  II. ADVICE (2:1-15)
 III. APPEAL (3:1-15)

DETAILED OUTLINE

   I. APPOINTMENTS (1:1-16)
     A. Approach (1:1-4)
       1. Position of Paul—A Servant and an Apostle (1:1)
       2. Privilege, Promise, and Preaching (1:2-3)
       3. Purpose and Person Who Received the Letter (1:4-5)

B. Assembly Matters (1:5-9)
   1. Attention to Any Emergency in the Churches (1:5)
   2. Appointment of Elders in Every City (1:5)
   3. Ability Required in an Elder (1:6-9)
      a. Negative
         (1) Not Self-willed
         (2) Not Soon Angry
         (3) Not a Winebibber
         (4) Not a Striker
         (5) Not a Seeker after Gain
      b. Positive
         (1) Blameless
         (2) Faithful Family
         (3) Hospitable
         (4) Friendly
         (5) Sober
         (6) Just
         (7) Holy
         (8) Even-tempered
         (9) Able to Exhort and Convince
C. Antagonists (1:10-16)
   1. Deceivers Subverting Many to Ways of Error (1:10-11)
   2. Dilatory and Careless of the Truth (1:12-13)
   3. Duped and Often Giving Heed to Fables (1:14)
   4. Defiled in Their Unbelief of the Truth (1:15)
   5. Denying the Lord Jesus in their Works (1:16)
   6. Disobedient and Unfit for His Work (1:16)

II. ADVICE (2:1-15)
   A. Regarding Sound Doctrine (2:1)
   B. Regarding Salient Duties (2:2-6,9-10)
      1. Soberness in All Things
      2. Soundness in Faith of All and in All
      3. Service of All and among All
   C. Regarding Sincere Deeds among Saints (2:11-15)
      1. Living a Regulated Life in Him (2:11-12)
      2. Looking for the Redeemer/Rapture (2:13)
      3. Leading Others to Righteousness (2:14-15)

III. APPEAL (3:1-15)
    A. Submission to Rulers in All Relevant Things (3:1)
    B. Showing Readiness for All Honorable Work (3:1-2)
    C. Slaves Redeemed from a Useless Past (3:3)
    D. Salvation and Renewal Now Ours to Enjoy (3:4-5)
    E. Sanctification Required and Provided in Him (3:6-8)
    F. Sundry Words of Wisdom in Conclusion (3:9-15)
        1. Admonition (3:9-11)
            a. Avoid Foolish Questions
            b. Avoid Fellowship with Heretics
            c. Accept the Facts
        2. Asking for Companions and Their Care (3:12-13)
        3. Asking for Continuance in Good Works (3:14)
        4. Adieu with Greetings in Love and Grace (3:15)

PHILEMON

NOTES

1. This short Epistle was written from Rome about A.D. 62-63.
2. It appears that when Tychicus took the letter of Paul to the church at Colossae, Onesimus took this letter to Philemon, who was probably an elder there (Philemon 2 and Colossians 4:7).
3. Archippus is mentioned in the Epistle to the Colossians (4:17) as well as in this Epistle (verse 2).
4. What John's second Epistle is to his writings, so this Epistle is to Paul's writings—a personal letter to a brother and friend asking a favor for someone else.

GENERAL OUTLINE

I. PROLOGUE (1-3)
II. LOVE'S APPRECIATION (4-7)
III. LOVE'S APPEAL (8-18)
IV. LOVE'S ASSURANCE (19-22)
V. EPILOGUE (23-25)

DETAILED OUTLINE

I. PROLOGUE (1-3)
   A. Personalities Addressed:
      1. Paul
      2. Timothy
      3. Philemon
      4. Apphia
      5. Archippus
      6. All the Saints
   B. Peace and Grace to All

II. LOVE'S APPRECIATION (4-7)
   A. Continual Remembrances in Prayer (4)
   B. Consecrated Relationships with the Lord (5)
   C. Conduct Recognized in Christ (6)
   D. Comforting Refreshment in Philemon's Love (7)

III. LOVE'S APPEAL (8-18)
   A. Entreaty (8-10)
      1. Boldness
      2. Bonds
      3. Birth of a Son
   B. Enlightenment (11-14)
      1. Record
      2. Representative
      3. Responsibility
   C. Enabling Grace of God (15-16)
      1. A Sinner Now Saved
      2. A Bondservant Now a Brother in Christ
   D. Enquiry (17-18)
      1. "If thou" a Partner
      2. "If he" a Pardoned Sinner

IV. LOVE'S ASSURANCE (19-22)
   A. Debt to Cancel (19)
   B. Deeds to Comfort (20)
   C. Desire to Come (21-22)

V. EPILOGUE (23-25)
   A. Fellow Prisoner
   B. Fellow Laborers
   C. Fellowship in Christ
   D. Fellowship with Christ

HEBREWS

NOTES

1. Neither the writer nor the recipients of this Epistle are named.
2. The Epistle was written to Hebrews who had become Christians and were in danger of returning to Judaism.
3. In form it is as much like a treatise as a letter.
4. No New Testament book is more occupied with the Lord Jesus Christ.
5. Hebrews records the immeasurable superiority of Christianity over Judaism, showing that the work of Christ fulfilled and substituted the Levitical sacrifices.
6. Hebrews is possibly the substance of Paul's preaching in Jewish synagogues. The thinking and argument is that of Paul, while the writing suggests that of Luke.
7. Note the following words:
    a. *Perfect* in one form or another is mentioned fourteen times
    b. *Eternal* occurs not less than fifteen times
    c. *Better* occurs thirteen times
    d. *Heavenly* or *Heaven* occurs seventeen times
8. Note *Christ* in Hebrews:
    a. His incarnation (1:2-5; 2:14; 7:14)
    b. His sinless humanity (4:15; 7:26)
    c. His temptations (2:18; 4:15)
    d. His ministry (1:2; 2:3)
    e. His agony (5:7)
    f. His cross (12:2; 13:12)
    g. His resurrection (13:20)
    h. His glorification (6:20; 7:1; 10:12)
    i. His return (9:28; 10:25,37)
9. Note the finality of the work of Christ:
    a. A sacrifice once (7:27)
    b. Entered into the holiest once (9:12)
    c. Appeared to put away sin once (9:26)
    d. Was offered once (9:28)
    e. Gave Himself once (10:10)

10. Note the superiority of Christ:
    a. Better than the angels (1:4)
    b. Better hope (7:19)
    c. Better testament (7:22)
    d. Better covenant on better promises (8:6)
    e. Better things or sacrifices (9:23)
    f. Better substance that is more enduring (10:34)
    g. Better country that is heavenly (11:16)
    h. Better resurrection (11:35)
    i. Better thing for us (6:9; 11:40)
    j. Better things speaking (12:24)

GENERAL OUTLINE

I. PERSONALITIES (1:1–7:28)
II. PORTRAITS OF THE PERSON (8:1–10:18)
III. PRACTICE (10:19–13:25)

DETAILED OUTLINE

I. PERSONALITIES (1:1–7:28)
   A. Christ and Angels (1:1-14)
      1. Savior and Lord (1:1-3)
         a. Messages God Spoke through Past Prophets (1:1)
         b. Majesty of Christ the Son an Exact Likeness (1:2-3)
         c. Manifestation of the Godhead Perfectly Expressed in Christ's Person and Work (1:3)
      2. Sanctified Loyalties of Angels (1:4-14)
         a. Christ the Son a More Excellent Name than They (1:4)
         b. Consider the Significance of Servants Not Sons (1:5-6)
         c. Condition As Subjects to Minister to God and Saints (1:7,14)
         d. Creator and Sovereign, Glory and Greatness (2:8-12)
         e. Contrasts of Servants and Saints (1:13-14)
   B. Saints and Sinners (2:1-18)
      1. Saints to Listen (2:1-4)

2. Apostasy to Avoid (10:26-31)
   a. Facts, "There remaineth no more sacrifice" (10:26)
   b. Fears for Those Who Despise His Work (10:27-29)
   c. Finality for All Such at His Hands (10:30-31)
3. Appeal for the Afflicted Ones (10:32-34)
   a. Remember the Endurance of Former Days (10:32)
   b. Reproaches Endured in Company with Others (10:33)
   c. Rest and Encouragement in Company with Others (10:34)
4. Anticipation of His Advent (10:35-39)
   a. Promise (10:36-37)
   b. Patience (10:35-36)
   c. Pleasure (10:38-39)

B. Hebrews 11
   Faith in a Superior Way
   1. Attitude of Faith (11:1-3)
      a. Substance
      b. Signs
      c. Sphere of Understanding
   2. Appropriation of Faith (11:4-40)
      a. Faith Honored by God—Abel to Abraham (11:4-16)
      b. Faith Honoring to God—Abraham to Moses (11:17-28)
      c. Faith Harnessed to the Power of God (11:29-34)
      d. Faithful Held in the Hands of God (11:35-38)
   3. Approved by Faith Providing Something Better (11:39-40)

C. Hebrews 12
   Fidelity in a Superior Work
   1. Admonition to Believers (12:1-11)
      a. Entreaty to Note (12:1)
         (1) Witnesses
         (2) Weights
         (3) Way
      b. Example of Christ (12:2-4)
         (1) Experience of Christ to Consider (12:2)
         (2) Enthronement of the Conqueror (12:2)
         (3) Encouragement from Christ to Follow (12:3-4)

   c. Endurance Called For—Discipline (12:5-8)
    (1) Deference to Elders (12:9-10)
    (2) Design in Production (12:11)
   d. Exhortation to the Believers (12:12-17)
    (1) Lending a Hand (12:12-14)
    (2) Looking Ahead (12:15)
    (3) Laying a Hazard of Profession without Possession (12:16-17)
  2. Approach on a Better Understanding (12:18-24)
   a. Under Mosaic Law—Experience of Fear (12:18-21)
    (1) Darkness (12:18)
    (2) Difficulty (12:18-20)
    (3) Dangers (12:20-21)
   b. Under Manifested Love—An Experience of Faith (12:22-24)
    (1) Great Angelic Company (12:22)
    (2) General Assembly (12:23)
    (3) God's Attested Covenant (12:24)
  3. Advice and a Warning Given (12:25-29)
   a. Refusal to Hear to Be Avoided (12:25)
   b. Resolve of God Adamant (12:26-27)
   c. Responsibility of Having Received—To Revere (12:28-29)
 D. Hebrews 13
  1. Steadfastness in Practice (13:1-9)
   a. Continuance in Love Called For (13:1-2)
   b. Conduct in Living among Believers (13:3-5)
   c. Confession of and for the Lord (13:6)
   d. Consideration of the Assembly Leaders (13:7-8)
   e. Confirmation of the Lessons Learned (13:9)
  2. Separation of His People (13:10-14)
   a. From the Figures of the Law—Tabernacle Worship (13:10-11)
   b. Fulfillment of Christ's Abiding Work—On Our Behalf (13:11-12)
   c. Following Christ Outside the Camp (13:13-14)
    (1) Camp behind Us—Separated From (13:13)
    (2) Companion Befriends Us—Bearing His Reproach (13:13)

(3) City before Us—Beckoning Ever Onward (13:14)
3. Sacrifice of Praise (13:15-16)
    a. Praise to God Continually for Everything (13:15)
    b. Privilege to Give Thanks in His Name (13:15)
    c. Pleasure to God in the Communication of His People (13:16)
4. Submission in Peace (13:17)
    a. Willingness
    b. Watchfulness
    c. Worthiness
5. Sympathetic Prayers (13:18-21)
    a. Intercession
    b. Intention
    c. Interest
6. Salutations (13:22-25)
    a. Beseeching the Brethren to Receive the Word (13:22)
    b. Bondage of Timothy At an End (13:23)
    c. Benediction and Greetings in Grace (13:24-25)

JAMES

NOTES

1. James was written to Jewish believers who were scattered abroad (James 1:1) about A.D. 50.
2. This Epistle is one of the so-called general Epistles; the others are 1 and 2 Peter, Jude, and 1 John.
3. James speaks of prayer and practice in the Christian life.
4. Paul and James were not opposite but apposite in their teaching. Paul attacked self-righteousness; James attacked barren orthodoxy.
5. The teaching of the sermon on the mount is reflected a great deal in this Epistle.
6. There are three well-known persons named James in the New Testament:
   a. James the brother of John, a son of Zebedee, who was called "the Greater" and was beheaded (Acts 12:2)
   b. James the son of Alphaeus, called "the Less"
   c. James the Lord's half-brother, called "the Just", who wrote this Epistle

GENERAL OUTLINE

I.   FAITH APPLIED IN TEMPTATION (1:1-27)
II. FAITH APPLIED IN TESTING TIMES (2:1-23)
III. FAITH APPLIED TO THE TONGUE (3:1-18)
IV. FAITH APPLIED TO THE TASK (4:1-17)
V.   FAITH APPLIED IN TRIUMPH (5:1-20)

DETAILED OUTLINE

I.   FAITH APPLIED IN TEMPTATION (1:1-27)
     A. Attitude of Faith (1:1-12)

      1. Prologue and Purpose in Temptations (1:1-2)
      2. Patience in Christian Experience (1:3-4)
      3. Perfecting of Character in Experience (1:4)
      4. Provision of Wisdom in Experience by Faith (1:6-8)
      5. Perseverance in Temptation with Promise (1:9-12)
   B. Argument for Faith (1:13-21)
      1. Consideration of Origins of Temptations (1:13-16)
      2. Contrast of His Gifts with Others (1:17-18)
      3. Concluding Reflection on Speed, Slowness, and Separation from Evil (1:19-21)
   C. Accord of Faith (1:22-25)
      1. Avoid Deception in Christian Living (1:22-23)
      2. Aim at Doing As We Hear from God (1:22, 24-25)
   D. Activity of Faith (1:26-27)
      1. Vanity of Deceptive Speeches (1:26)
      2. Visitation of the Saints in Need (1:27)
      3. Victory of a Separated Life of Faith (1:27)

II. FAITH APPLIED IN TESTING TIMES (2:1-23)
   A. Right Way among the Lord's People (2:1-9)
      1. Concern for Each Other Impartial (2:1,4)
      2. Clothes of Each Other Immaterial (2:2-3)
      3. Care for Each Other Intentional (2:5)
      4. Conduct toward Each Other Impeccable (2:6-9)
   B. Responsibility of Witness (2:10-19)
      1. Violation of God's Laws Brings Judgment (2:10-13)
      2. Validity of Faith with Works Evident (2:14-15)
      3. Vanity of Faith without Works Evident (2:16-19)
   C. Righteous Works of Faith Displayed (2:20-26)
      1. Implementation of Faith with Works Brings Fruitfulness (2:20-21)
      2. Justification by Faith and Works Illustrated (2:22-26)
      3. Imputation of Righteousness to Abraham (2:23)

III. FAITH APPLIED TO THE TONGUE (3:1-18)
   A. Perils Indicated (3:1-8)
      1. Teachers' Problems in Daily Walk and Talk (3:1-2)
      2. Twofold Analogy of Control (3:3-4)
         a. Horses
         b. Ships

B. Patience in Experience among Believers (5:7-12)
   1. Anticipation of Fruitfulness (5:7)
      a. Wait
      b. Watch
      c. Work
   2. Advent of the Judge to Call to Account (5:8-9)
   3. Assurance Given to Those Who Endure (5:11)
   4. Answering All with Decision and Clarity (5:12)
C. Prayer to Emulate in Daily Exercise (5:13-20)
   1. Sick among the Lord's People (5:13-16)
   2. Success in Prayer Illustrated—Elijah (5:17-18)
   3. Salvation of the Erring Ones from Ruin (5:19-20)

1 PETER

NOTES

1. The Epistles of First and Second Peter were written to Jewish believers who were scattered abroad (1 Peter 1:1; 2 Peter 3:1).
2. They are known as general Epistles; the others being James, 1 John, and Jude.
3. Both these Epistles mention Noah (1 Peter 3:20; 2 Peter 2:5).
4. Peter records his own witness of Christ (1 Peter 5:1); and speaks of his own experiences (cf. 1 Peter 5:2 with John 21:16 and 2 Peter 1:16-17 with Matthew 17:1-6).
5. These Epistles were probably written during Nero's reign.
6. The purpose of both appears to be to exhort, comfort and strengthen the believers.
7. Peter lays special stress on the believer's moral obligation to the law of God and to Christ's coming again.
80. These Epistles were probably written from Rome about A.D. 64-65.

GENERAL OUTLINE

   I. SALVATION (1:1-2:8)
  II. SUBMISSION (2:9-3:12)
 III. SUFFERING (3:13-4:9)
  IV. SERVICE (4:1-5:14)

DETAILED OUTLINE

   I. SALVATION (1:1-2:8)
      A. Greetings (1:1-2)
         1. Countries in Which the Believers Were (1:10)
         2. Chosen of God; the Trinity Involved (1:2)

B. Giving Thanks to God. (1:3-5)
1. Person of Christ; His Work and Resurrection (1:3)
2. Prospect of an Inheritance in Heaven (1:4)
3. Power to Be Kept Now and for a Coming Day (1:5)

C. Glory of Christ; A Background to Earthly Trials (1:1:6-9)
1. Testing Days Ahead to Try Believers (1:6-7)
2. Trusting Faith Precious in God's Sight (1:6-7)
3. Testimony of Living Faith in Him (1:8-9)

D. Gospel of Christ (1:10-21)
1. Report of the Prophets (i.e. Isaiah 53) (1:10)
2. Revelation of God the Holy Spirit (1:11-12)
3. Reception by Those Who Obey the Truth (1:13-17)
4. Redemption by Christ At So Great a Cost (1:18-21)

E. Grace of God in the Gospel (1:22-25)
1. In Obeying the Truth of It (1:22)
2. In the Obligations of the Practice Thereof (1:22-23)
3. In the Operation of the Gospel Continually (1:25)

F. Goodness in the Gospel (2:1-8)
1. Goodness in Preference to Guile among Believers (2:1-3)
2. Grounded Firmly on the Foundation of Christ (2:4-6)
3. Growing Up on That Foundation (2:5-8)

II. SUBMISSION (2:9–3:12)
A. Chosen of God in Christ (2:9)
1. Priesthood with a Royal Status
2. People for His Own Possession
3. Purpose to Show Forth His Praise

B. Conduct of Those Thus Chosen (2:10-12)
1. Attainment through Grace (2:10)
2. Absent from Enemy Activity, As Pilgrims (2:11)
3. Attesting to Good Works in Glorifying His Name (2:12)

C. Commitment to the Will of God (2:13-25)
1. Cause Shown: "For the Lord's sake" (2:13)
2. Character: "For so is the will of God" (2:14-17)
3. Conduct Therein: "For this is thankworthy" (2:18-20)
4. Call to Follow Christ's Example: "Christ also" (2:21-25)

D. Concern of All Involved (3:1-11)
1. Spirit of Submission (3:1-6)

      a. Motive: Won by the Wives (3:1)

      b. Message on Behavior: Chaste Conversation (3:2)

      c. Manner of Behavior: Inward Not Outward (3:3-4)

      d. Many Examples Who Have Passed On (3:5-6)

  2. Spirit of Sincerity (3:7)

      a. Honor

      b. Heirs

      c. Happiness Together

  3. Spirit of Service (3:8-11)

      a. Love: Compassion and Sympathy Expressed (3:8)

      b. Hospitality One to Another Generously (3:9)

      c. Giving What We Have Received As Good Stewards (3:10)

      d. Ministry according to the Ability Given Us (3:11-12)

III. SUFFERING (3:13–4:9)

  A. Confidence of the Christian (3:12)

    1. Eyes of the Lord on His Own

    2. Ears of the Lord Open to His Own

    3. Face of the Lord Opposed to Evildoers

  B. Case for the Christian (3:13-17)

    1. Possibility of Suffering (3:13-14)

    2. Personal Sanctity (3:15)

      a. Approach

      b. Answer

      c. Attitude

    3. Peace Even in Suffering—He Is There (Matthew 28:20) (3:16-17)

  C. Conduct of Christ (3:18-22)

    1. Lord's Passion and Its Purpose (3:18)

    2. Lord's Proclamation to the Prisoners (3:19-20)

    3. Lord's Proof in Picture-form—Baptism (3:21)

    4. Lord's Position of Power in Heaven (3:22)

  D. Challenge to Christians (4:1-6)

    1. Fellowship with Christ (4:1)

    2. Fidelity to Christ (4:2)

    3. Foolishness of Men (4:3-4)

    4. Fairness to All (4:5-6)

    5. Faithfulness to Each Other (4:7-9)

IV. SERVICE (4:10–5:14)
   A. Stewardship Involved according to Ability Given (4:10-11)
   B. Servant Identified with Him in His Service (4:12-19)
      1. Rejoicing as Partakers with Him (4:12-13)
      2. Reproach for Christ's Sake (Hebrews 13:12-13) (4:14-16)
      3. Resource in the Will of God for All (4:17-19)
   C. Sincere Incentive to Serve Willingly (5:1-3)
   D. Shepherd's Inspiration in Present Service Worthy of Him with Promise of Coming Reward (5:4)
   E. Submission Invited in a Spirit of Humility One to Another (5:5-6)
   F. Strength Imparted by the God of All Grace to Combat Every Artifice of the Evil One (5:7-11)
   G. Salutations in Conclusion (5:12-14)
      1. Silas
      2. Mark
      3. Peter

2 Peter

Notes

1. This Epistle was probably written from Rome shortly after the first Epistle of Peter around A.D. 65.
2. The words "remember," "keep," and "knowledge" occur again and again in the second Epistle of Peter.
3. Peter records the prophecy of Christ to his own death (2 Peter 1:14).

General Outline

I. CHARACTER DESIRED (1:1-21)
II. CONFLICT DESCRIBED (2:1-22)
III. CONSUMMATION DETAILS (3:1-18)

Detailed Outline

I. CHARACTER DESIRED (1:1-21)
   A. Salutations to the People of God (1:1-2)
      1. The Righteousness of God
      2. Grace and Peace
   B. Sufficient Provision Made by Him (1:3-4)
      1. Power for All the Needs of Life and Godliness (1:3)
      2. Precious Promises on Which to Rest our Souls (1:4)
      3. Partakers of His Divine Nature (1:4)
   C. Successful Progress Possible to All in Him (1:5-11)
      1. Additions in Christian Experience (1:5-7)
      2. Advance in Knowledge and Practices (1:8-9)
      3. Admonition to Be Diligent in Exercise (1:10)
      4. Abundant Entrance Assured Us (1:11)
   D. Satisfying Presence of Christ (1:12-21)
      1. Invoking the Memory (1:12-15)

        a. Concerning the Past

        b. Concerning the Future

    2. Identity with the Majesty of His Person (1:16-18)

    3. Inspiration of the Message for Our Mutual Profit (1:19-21)

II. CONFLICT DESCRIBED (2:1-22)

    A. Doctrine Defined of the Antagonists to Truth (2:1-3)

        1. False Teachers to Be Found among Believers (2:1)

        2. Fatal Teaching—Denying the Lord Himself (2:1)

        3. Followers Trapped by Such Evil Teaching (2:2-3)

    B. Destruction Declared As Certain (2:3-9)

        1. Not Sleeping—Their Ruin Certain (2:3)

        2. Not Sparing—Even the Angels or the Ancients (2:4-5)

        3. Not Saving—Even As Sodom and Gomorrha (2:6-9)

    C. Doings Described—To Their Undoing (2:10-22)

        1. Reserved for Punishment—All the Unjust (2:9-10)

        2. Rewarded for Presumption—All the Unclean (2:10-14)

        3. Rebuke for a Prophet—A Way of Unrighteousness (2:15-16)

        4. Reckless Pretence—Words with Emptiness (2:17-18)

        5. Retribution for the Polluted—Promises without Performance (2:19-22)

III. CONSUMMATION DETAILS (3:1-18)

    A. Lord's Return Assailed (3:1-4)

        1. Quest for Pure Minds to Remember (3:1)

        2. Quotations from Prophetic Messages (3:2)

        3. Question:"Where is the promise?" (3:3-4)

    B. Lord's Return Attested (3:5-10)

        1. Creation Perished under a Past Judgment (3:5-6)

        2. Coming Perdition Inevitable Now As Then (3:7)

        3. Concerning the Promise—"The Lord is not slack" (3:8-10)

    C. Lord's Return Anticipated (3:11-18)

        1. Diligence Called For in All Walks of Life (3:11-14)

        2. Discernment Called For in Understanding the Word (3:15-16)

        3. Devotion Called For in Continuing Steadfast in the Lord (3:17-18)

1 John

Notes

1. John was one of the first to follow the Lord and the last to pass away among the apostles.
2. His life spanned almost the entire first century.
3. His writings are only second to Paul's in quantity and importance to the Christian church.
4. The first Epistle was probably written from Ephesus about A.D. 90-96.
5. Polycarp, A.D. 116, who knew John, confirms that John was the writer of this Epistle. Papias, A.D. 120, and Irenaeus, A.D. 175, also confirm this fact.
6. Three heresies arose in the early church:
   a. Ebionites who denied the Lord's deity
   b. Docetists who denied the Lord's humanity
   c. Cerenthians who denied the union of the Lord's two natures before baptism
7. These errors were met by this Epistle (1 John 1:1-3; 4:3,15; 5:1, etc.).
8. Two other errors are also dealt with here:
   a. Sinless perfection (1 John 1:8-10)
   b. Antinomianism: those that considered they could live as they pleased without obligation to the moral law (1 John 1:3-9; 2:1-6)

General Outline

I. Fellowship in the Lord (1:1-4)
II. Fellowship in Light (1:5-2:29)
III. Fellowship in Love (3:1-4:21)
IV. Fellowship in Life (5:1-21)

Detailed Outline

I. FELLOWSHIP IN THE LORD (1:1-4)
   A. Means of Fellowship—The Incarnation (1:1)
      1. Hearing
      2. Seeing
      3. Handling
   B. Manifestation of His Life Made Known to Faith (1:2)
   C. Motive Revealed (1:3-4)
      1. Fellowship with the Father (1:3)
      2. Fullness of Joy (1:4)

II. FELLOWSHIP IN LIGHT (1:5–2:29)
   A. Privilege to Walk in the Light (1:5-7)
      1. Declaring That God Is the Essence of Light (1:5)
      2. Deception to Be Avoided—Say and Do the Same (1:6)
      3. Delights of Fellowship One with Another (1:7)
   B. Position of the Believer (1:8-10)
      1. "If" of Conceit (1:8)
      2. "If" of Confession (1:9)
      3. "If" of Contrariness (1:10)
   C. Provision for Times of Need (2:1-6)
      1. Advocate—Sin the Exception Not the Practice (2:1-2)
      2. Adherence to the Truth in Him (2:3-5)
      3. Abiding in Him Produces a Likeness in Walk (2:6)
   D. Practice of Walking in the Light (2:7-10)
      1. Demonstrates an Old Commandment
      2. Developed on a Basis of Love
   E. Perils for the Believer (2:11-23)
      1. Of the Wicked One (2:11-14)
         a. Children
         b. Young Men
         c. Fathers
      2. Of the World (2:15-17)
         a. Love
         b. Lust
         c. Pride
      3. Of the Will of Men Contrary to the Will of God (2:18-23)
         a. Danger Ahead with Many Antichrists (2:18)

b. Divisions Resulting in Infidelity to Him (2:19)

c. Denials That Follow (2:20-23)

F. Promise to Those Who Abide in Him (2:24-29)

   1. Continuity of Abiding with Promise (2:24-25)

   2. Consecrated Anointing of the Lord (2:26-27)

   3. Confidence in Him and His Appearing (2:28-29)

III. FELLOWSHIP IN LOVE (3:1-4:21)

A. Privilege of His Love (3:1)

   1. Fact

   2. Feature

   3. Foes

B. Perfection in Love (3:2)

   1. Relationship—Sons

   2. Revelation—When He Appears

   3. Reality—Like Him

C. Purity in Loving Him (3:3)

   1. Scope

   2. State

   3. Savior

D. Practice of Sin a Practice of Lawlessness (3:4)

E. Person Who Loved (3:5)

   1. His Advent

   2. His Ability

   3. His Authority

F. Power of Love (3:6)

   1. Condition of That Power

   2. Consequence of That Abiding

   3. Contrast with Abiding

G. Precaution in Love (3:7-8)

   1. Suggestion—Let No Man Deceive

   2. Substance in Resistance—His Righteousness

   3. Source of Evil—The Devil

H. Purpose in Love Manifested (3:8)

   1. Deity of Christ—The Son Manifest in the Flesh

   2. Destruction of Satan's Works

I. Provision Made in Love (3:9)

   1. New Birth

   2. New Blessing

   3. New Behavior

J. Proof of Love in Deeds—Negatively (3:10)
No Love for One Another
K. Proof of Love in Deeds—"Love one another" (3:11)
L. Proofs of Love That Follow (3:12-24)
  1. Contrast to Avoid (3:12-13)
  2. Certainty to Acknowledge (3:14-15)
    a. Fact
    b. Fruit
    c. Fate
  3. Challenge to Accept (3:16-21)
    a. Christ's Example (3:16)
    b. Compassion Expressed (3:17)
    c. Christian Exercise (3:18)
    d. Comfort in Experience (3:19)
    e. Conduct Exemplified (3:20-21)
  4. Conclusion to Aim For (3:22-24)
    a. Keeping and Doing
    b. Believing and Loving
    c. Dwelling and Abiding
M. Personality of Love (4:1-21)
  1. Menace to Love (4:1-6)
    a. Danger of Evil and Seducing Spirits (4:1)
    b. Discernment of Truth and Error (4:2-3)
    c. Defeat of the Adversary by Christ in Us (4:4)
    d. Division between the Spirit of Truth and Error (4:5-6)
  2. Magnitude of Love (4:7-10)
    a. Origin of Love—From God (4:7)
    b. Essence of Love—God Himself (4:8)
    c. Miracle of Love—He Loved Us (4:9-10)
  3. Meaning of Love (4:11-21)
    a. Testimony in Daily Living (4:11-15)
    b. Truth and Fruit without Fear (4:16-19)
    c. Its Test among Believers (4:20-21)

IV. FELLOWSHIP IN LIFE (5:1-21)
  A. The Declaration—Whosoever Believeth (5:1)
    1. The Facts
    2. The Fraternity—Mutual Love and Obedience (5:2-3)
    3. The Faith—Victory over the World (5:4-5)

B. Details of a Threefold Witness (5:6-8)
C. Definition of the Truth (5:9-12)
   1. Witness of Man and God (5:9)
   2. Witness within the Heart (5:10)
   3. Witness of the Word of Truth (5:11-12)
D. Desire of the Apostle John (5:13-21)
   1. Purpose in Writing to Them (5:13)
   2. Prayers of the Saints according to His Will (5:14-17)
   3. Position of the Saints in Christ (5:18-20)
   4. Plea to Guard against Idols (5:21)

2 JOHN

NOTES

1. This letter was probably written from Ephesus about A.D. 90-96.
2. Second John is in John's writings what Philemon is in Paul's.
3. This short Epistle speaks much of home and hospitality.
4. It is concerned with truth and the believer's walk in declining days, and includes an expressed wish to see them.

GENERAL OUTLINE

  I. PATHWAY OF TRUTH (1-6)
 II. PERILS AND TESTING (7-11)
III. POSTSCRIPT AND A TRYST (12-13)

DETAILED OUTLINE

  I. PATHWAY OF TRUTH (1-6)
    A. Devotion and Love to the Lady and the Saints (1)
    B. Dwelling Place of Truth—Within (2)
    C. Displayed Gifts of God (3)
      1. Grace
      2. Mercy
      3. Peace
    D. Delight in and Desire to Walk in Love (4-6)

 II. PERILS AND TESTING (7-11)
    A. Deceivers Abroad Doing Their Evil Work (7)
    B. Discernment Called for among Believers (8)
    C. Doctrine of the Lord a Testing Point (9)
    D. Defaulters Not to Be Received by Believers (10-11)

III. POSTSCRIPT AND A TRYST (12-13)
   A. Concern for Them Evident (12)
   B. Coming to Them a Real Desire (12)
   C. Contentment in Seeing Them Face to Face (12)
   D. Conclusion in Greetings Sent (13)

3 John

Notes

1. This Epistle was probably written about A.D. 90-96.
2. It is the shortest letter in the New Testament—295 words in the Authorized Version.
3. The letter was written to Gaius who was in a church possibly founded by John himself.
4. There are three of the same name in the New Testament—at Corinth (1 Corinthians 1:14), at Macedonia (Acts 19:29), and at Derbe (Acts 20:4-5).
5. It is possible that the recipient of this letter was one of them.
6. Diotrephes was a contrasting character in the same assembly.

General Outline

I. DEDICATION AND GAIUS (1-8)
II. DIOTREPHES AND GREED (9-10)
III. DEMETRIUS AND GOODNESS (11-12)
IV. DESIRES AND GREETINGS (13-14)

Detailed Outline

I. DEDICATION AND GAIUS (1-8)
   A. Well-beloved of the Aged Elder and Apostle (1)
   B. Well-wisher to Gaius Evidently a Faithful Man (2)
   C. Well-reported by Those Who Knew Him Best (3)
   D. Well-being in Walk, Faith, and Truth (5-8)
      1. Activities among the Lord's People (5-6)
      2. Allegiance to Christ (7)
      3. Association with Others Likeminded (8)

II. DIOTREPHES AND GREED (9-10)
   A. Pride—A Place-Seeker Who Sought Preeminence (9)
   B. Perversion of Truth against Other Believers (10)
   C. Presumption in Dividing the Lord's People (10)

III. DEMETRIUS AND GOODNESS (11-12)
   A. Wish and Good Advice of the Apostle (11)
   B. Worker Whom All Men Knew for His Work (12)
   C. Witness of the Elder Himself Added Thereto (12)

IV. DESIRES AND GREETINGS (13-14)
   A. Send a Word in Writing to Them (13)
   B. Speak with Them Face to Face (14)
   C. Salute Them with Peace in Greeting (14)

JUDE

NOTES

1. There are six with the name of Jude or Judas in the New Testament:
   a. Jude, the brother of James, half-brother to Christ (Jude 1:1, Matthew 13:55, Mark 6:3)
   b. Judas, brother of another apostle, James (Luke 6:16, John 14:22)
   c. Judas of Galilee (Acts 5:37)
   d. Judas of Damascus (Acts 9:11)
   e. Judas of the name Barsabas, an elder (Acts 15:22,27)
   f. Judas Iscariot, who betrayed the Lord
2. The purpose of this Epistle appears to be to denounce and warn against the pernicious errors which were spreading at that time (Jude 3).
3. Note the recurrence of "threes" in this Epistle:
   a. Salutation: Sanctified—preserved—called (1)
   b. Benediction: Mercy—peace—love (2)
   c. Retribution: Israel—angels—Sodomites
   d. Wickedness: Cain—Balaam—Korah (11)
   e. People: Murmurers—complainers—proud
   f. Exhortation: Building—keeping—looking
   g. Commendation: To keep—to present—to joy (24)
   h. Illustration: Shepherds (no love)—clouds (no water)—trees (no fruit)

GENERAL OUTLINE

I. RELATIONSHIP AND THE REASON FOR WRITING (1-4)
II. REMEMBRANCE AND THE RESULTS (5-19)
III. RESPONSE AND REASSURANCE GIVEN (20-25)

DETAILED OUTLINE

I. RELATIONSHIP AND THE REASON FOR WRITING (1-4)
   A. Detail of Personal Relationship with James, Therefore with Christ after the Flesh (1-2)
      1. A Brother
      2. A Bond
      3. A Blessing
   B. Duty to Write and to Contend for the Faith (3)
   C. Danger to Combat within the Church (4)
      1. Men Referred to Were Ungodly
      2. Methods Were Secret
      3. Mischief Was the Denial of the Lord Jesus Christ

II. REMEMBRANCE AND THE RESULTS (5-19)
   A. Destruction of Apostasy for Israelites Who Sinned (5)
   B. Darkness for Angels Who Made Such a Choice (6)
   C. Doom of Apostates Such As Sodom and Gomorrha (7)
   D. Dreamers of Filth—Corrupt with No Conscience (8)
   E. Despisers of Worthy Persons and Laws (8)
   F. Dispute according to Knowledge or Ignorance (9-10)
   G. Demonstration of Such by Three People (11-13)
      1. Cain, the Murderer (Genesis 4:8) (11)
      2. Balaam, the Peddler of Error (Numbers 31:16) (11)
      3. Korah, the Rebel against Authority (Numbers 16:8-10) (11)
      4. An Illustrated Description of All Such (12-13)
   H. Disclosure of Coming Events (14-19)
      1. Conviction of Coming Judgments by Enoch (14-15)
      2. Complaint of Self-centered Christ Rejectors (16)
      3. Criticism of Sensual Mockers in the Last Days (17-19)

III. RESPONSE AND REASSURANCE GIVEN (20-25)
   A. Devotion of Believers in Building Up Their Faith (20)
   B. Discipline of Continuing in Life and Love of God (21)
   C. Dedication in Witness and Compassionate Conviction (22-23)
   D. Destination of All True Believers in Christ (24-25)
      1. Able to Preserve
      2. Able to Present

REVELATION

NOTES

1. This is perhaps the greatest of all the prison Epistles.
2. It was probably written about A.D. 96 by John the apostle and writer of the Gospel and Epistles that bear his name.
3. It was written to seven churches in Asia Minor, yet with a living message to every church everywhere.
4. It is "The Revelation of Jesus Christ" (1:1), and speaks much of Him, i.e., the Lamb, the Bridegroom, the King, etc.
5. A brief analysis is seen in Revelation 1:19:
    a. Write: "Things which thou hast seen" (chapter 1)
    b. Write: "Things which are" (chapters 2-3)
    c. Write: "Things which shall be hereafter" (chapters 4-22)
        • Chapters 4-18 suggest events between the rapture and the millennium
        • Chapters 19:1-20:6 suggest events during the millennium
        • Chapters 20:7-22:21 suggest events after the millennium
6. There are four main lines of interpretation to the book:
    a. Preterist: That this book deals with the first century only
    b. Historical: That this book deals with history between the advents
    c. Spiritual: That this book deals with symbolic light and dark
    d. Futurist: That this book deals with coming events, last days, and things yet to be
7. Note that the word "shortly" (Revelation 1:1) should be translated "quickly" or "speedily" as *tachei* from *tachus* is so translated seven times in Revelation (2:5,16; 3:11; 11:14; 22:7,12, 20).
8. The seven seals reveal:
    a. A white horse
    b. A red horse
    c. A black horse
    d. A pale horse
    e. Souls of martyrs

    f. An earthquake and an eclipse

    g. Silence

9. The seven trumpets reveal:

    a. Plagues on the earth

    b. Plagues on the sea

    c. Plagues on the rivers

    d. An eclipse

    e. Invasion of locusts

    f. Raid of horsemen

    g. A heavenly chorus in triumphant praise

10. The seven vials reveal:

    a. Plagues on the earth

    b. Plagues on the sea

    c. Plagues on springs and rivers

    d. Plague on the sun

    e. Plague on the beast's kingdom

    f. Plague on the river Euphrates

    g. Plague in the air

11. Note the repetition of the number "seven" in this book.

12. No other book speaks more often of angels.

13. John is told to "write" twelve times and "write...not" once.

14. John says "I heard" twenty-seven times in this book and uses "saw" or "behold" forty-four times.

15. The fourth seal speaks of the death of a quarter of the world's population. The sixth trumpet speaks of the death of a further third of the world's population.

GENERAL OUTLINE

  I. PAST (1:1-20)

 II. PRESENT (2:1-3:22)

III. PREDICTIVE (4:1-22:21)

DETAILED OUTLINE

  I. PAST (1:1-20)

    A. Angel and the Scribe (1:1-3)

1. Revelation of the Lord Jesus (1:1)
   a. Who Sent His Angel to John at Patmos
   b. Who Showed John What Would Take Place Quickly
   c. Who Signified the Same with Signs
2. Record of the Word (1:2)
   a. Truth of God's Word
   b. Testimony of the Lord Jesus Himself
   c. Things Seen and Recorded by John
3. Reading of the Word of God (1:3)
   a. Receiving the Word and Hearing Its Message
   b. Retaining the Message—Holding It in Mind and Heart
   c. Resulting in Blessing to the Reader
B. Assemblies in Asia (1:4-5)
   1. Seven Churches, Typical of Churches Everywhere (1:4)
   2. Salutations to the Churches from Christ Himself (1:4)
   3. Savior Who Knew and Was Known by John (1:4-5)
      a. Faithful Witness (Acts 1:8)
      b. Firstborn from the Dead
      c. First among Rulers over All Others
C. Ascription of Praise (1:5-7)
   1. Freedom from the Penalty of Sins (1:5)
   2. Formation of Priests and Kings for Himself (1:6)
   3. Future Glory for the Lord Jesus Predicted (1:6-7)
      a. Dominion (1:6)
      b. Descent (1:7)
      c. Dejection of Men (1:7)
D. Alpha and Omega (1:8)
   1. Redeemer—In This He Was Unique
   2. Resident—In Every True Believer
   3. Ruler—Invincible and Almighty
E. Attestation of John (1:9-11)
   1. Companionship with the Saints in Times of Trouble (1:9)
   2. Comprehension of the Voice of the Holy Spirit (1:10)
   3. Command to See and Send the Record to the Churches (1:11)
F. The Appearance to John (1:12-16)
   1. The Seven Golden Candlesticks and a Voice (1:12)

2. Son of Man in the Center—Clothed, with Shining Countenance (1:13-16)
3. Seven Stars in His Hand—A Sign of Control (1:16)
4. Sharp Sword in His Mouth—A Sign of Power (1:16)

G. Assurance Given to John (1:17-20)
    1. Prostration of John at the Sight of Him (1:17)
    2. Power to Revive and Refresh John (1:17-18)
    3. Plan Revealed to John (1:19)
        a. Past
        b. Present
        c. Future
    4. Perplexity Explained to John by the Lord Himself (1:20)

II. PRESENT (2:1–3:22)

A. Church at Ephesus (2:1-7)
    1. Declaration by Christ As He Walks among the Churches (2:1)
    2. Deeds Known (2:2-3)
        a. Dedication
        b. Detection
        c. Devotion
    3. Declension in This Second Generation of Believers Evident (2:4)
        a. Drifting from Their First Love
        b. Departure from Their First Love
    4. Danger—A Warning Given to Them (2:5)
        a. Remember
        b. Repent
        c. Be Removed
    5. Dividing Influence of the Nicolaitanes Opposed (2:6)
    6. Delight in Being an Overcomer (2:7)

B. Church at Smyrna (2:8-11)
    1. Command of Authority to the Recipients—Record from One Who Was Dead but Is Alive (2:8)
    2. Circumstances of Activity of the Church (2:9)
        a. Private Affairs
            (1) Work
            (2) Want
            (3) Wealth

        b. Public Antagonists
           (1) Misrepresentation
           (2) Misapprehension
           (3) Misfortune
    3. Comfort in Adversity for Them All (2:10)
    4. Confident Assurance for Hearers Who Overcome
       (2:11)

C. Church at Pergamos (2:12-17)
    1. Sword Conditioned for Use When Needed (2:12)
    2. Seat in Contrast to That of the Faithful (2:13)
        a. Dwelling with Difficulties
        b. Dedication without Denial by Antipas
        c. Devotion to Christ Desired
    3. Stumbling Block in Compromise with Evil (2:14)
    4. Separation by Consent from the Evils of Nicolaitanes
       (2:15)
    5. Sentence against the Church at Pergamos (2:16)
        a. Repentance or Alternative
        b. Rectify the Aims of the Church—Unity Not Disunity
        c. Repudiation of Balaamism and the Nicolaitanes
    6. Sign to Comfort Those Who Will Hear (2:17)

D. Church at Thyatira (2:18-29)
    1. Observation of the Lord (2:18-19)
        a. Word to Say
        b. Way to Walk
        c. Wealth of Work
    2. Opposition Voiced by the Lord
        a. Sufferance of Jezebel to Teach
        b. Seduction by Her to Her Teaching
        c. Sin in Allowing Such a State to Be
    3. Opportunity Given (2:21)
        a. No Argument about Repentance Required
        b. No Alternative Offered to Repentance
        c. No Acceptance in Repentance by Her
    4. Operation of the Justice of God (2:22-23)
        a. Retribution—Sin Dealt with Impartially (2:22)
        b. Revelation—Secrets All Known to Him (2:22)
        c. Rewards—Sowing of the Seed (2:23)
    5. Overcomers Have Their Own Blessing (2:24-29)
        a. Dedication to, and with, the Truth (2:24)

 b. Devotion to Hold the Truth till He Come (2:25)
 c. Declaration to the Faithful Who Overcome (2:26-29)
  (1) Conditions (2:26)
  (2) Co-heirship with Christ (2:27-28)
  (3) Challenge (2:29)
E. Church at Sardis (3:1-6)
 1. Message to a People with a Tradition (3:1)
  a. Recipients—A People with a Name
  b. Remarks of Him Who Observed Their Work
  c. Reproach of Having a Name to Live yet Be Dead
 2. Malady in the Church (3:2-3)
  a. Decay—They Were Ready to Die (3:2)
  b. Drift—They Were Not What They Used to Be (3:2)
  c. Duty—To Remember, Repent, and Watch (3:2)
  d. Danger—To Remedy the Malady or Pay the Price (3:3)
 3. Means to Achieve (3:4-5)
  a. To Be Washed and Clothed—Purity in Standing (3:4-5)
  b. To Walk and Confirm the Power Available (3:4-5)
  c. To Be Worthy—Confessed by Him before God (3:5-6)
F. Church at Philadelphia (3:7-13)
 1. Correspondent—His Identity (3:7)
 2. Commendation to Faithful Witnesses (3:8)
  a. Deeds
  b. Door
  c. Dependence
  d. Devotion
 3. Conflict with the Jews of That Day (3:9)
  a. Apostates Coerced to Come and Worship
  b. Assumed Conceit
  c. Altogether Convinced
 4. Comfort of Faith and Fellowship with Him (3:10-11)
  a. Dedication to a Task (3:10)
  b. Deliverance from Temptation (3:10)
  c. Defence of the Truth (3:11)
 5. Confidence for, and of, the Overcomer (3:12-13)
  a. A Pillar as an Abiding Erection
  b. A Peace as an Abiding Enjoyment

      c. A Privilege as an Abiding Experience

      d. A Power through an Abiding Exercise

G. Church at Laodicea (3:14-22)

  1. Controller (3:14)

      a. Angel of the Church

      b. Amen, the Faithful

      c. Attestation Given

      d. Author of All Creation

  2. Condition (3:15-17)

      a. Works Only External (3:15)

        (1) Lukewarm

        (2) Lifeless

      b. Wealth Rich yet Wretched (3:16)

        (1) Affluent

        (2) Autonomous

      c. Woes Evident (3:17)

        (1) Ignorance

        (2) Indifference

  3. Counsel (3:18)

      a. Purchases Needed by Them

        (1) Gold

        (2) White Raiment

        (3) Eye Salve

      b. Person Who Will Provide for Them

      c. Purpose of the Purchases

  4. Call (3:19-20)

      a. Rebuke on a Basis of Love for Them (3:19)

      b. Repentance Required of Them by the Lord

      c. Restraint of the One outside the Door (3:20)

      d. Reception to Be from Within (3:20)

      e. Response Certain from Him (3:20)

  5. Conclusion (3:21-22)

      a. Exhortation to Overcome with Its Promise (3:21)

      b. Example of Christ's Triumph in Overcoming (3:21)

      c. Ear to Hear—To Accept the Responsibility (3:22)

III. PREDICTIVE (4:1-22:21)

A. Scene in Heaven (4:1-5:14)

  1. Venue in Heaven (4:1)

  2. Voice of the Son of Man (4:1)

3. Vision of the Throne (4:2-11)
   a. Occupant of the Throne (4:2-3)
   b. Others Seated on Twenty-four Thrones (4:4)
   c. Observation of John At What He Saw (5:5-11)
      (1) Concerning the Phenomena
         (a) Voices
         (b) Lamps
         (c) Seven Spirits
      (2) Creatures—Eyes Before and Behind (4:6)
      (3) Characteristics of the Creature (Ezekiel 1:10) (4:7-8)
      (4) Confession of the Creatures and Elders (4:9-11)
4. Victor (5:1-5)
   a. Sealed Book
   b. Strong Angel
   c. Sorrow Silenced
5. Verdict (5:6-14)
   a. Lamb Worthy to Open the Book (5:6-7)
   b. Loyal Worship of the Hosts of Heaven (5:8-12)
   c. Lion-Lamb—The Wonder of All Creation (5:13-14)
      (1) Redeemed Sing (5:9-10)
      (2) Angels Speak (5:12)
      (3) Residue Praise and Bless Him (5:13-14)
B. Six Seals (6:1-17)
   1. First Seal—The White Horse (6:1-2)
      a. Command to Come
      b. Crown
      c. Conqueror
   2. Second Seal—The Red Horse (6:4)
      a. Sword
      b. Strife
      c. Suffering
   3. Third Seal—The Black Horse (6:5-6)
      a. Balances for Us in a Coming Time of Famine (6:5)
      b. Bread and Barley—Food for Rich and Poor (6:6)
      c. Bitterness Resulting from Such Injustices (6:6)
   4. Fourth Seal—The Pale Horse (6:7-8)
      a. Freedom to Kill Given Them—Death and Hell to Follow

    d. Fourth Trumpet (8:12-13)
      (1) Darkened Light from Smitten Sun, Moon, and Stars
      (2) Daylight Diminished by a Third
      (3) Danger Ahead for Earth Dwellers
      (4) Three Woes to Come
    e. Fifth Trumpet (9:1-12)
      (1) Star from Heaven Falls (9:1)
      (2) Smoke from a Furnace Darkens the Sky (9:2)
      (3) Sting like a Scorpion from a Locust (9:3)
      (4) Seal—God's Safety Device for His Own (9:4)
      (5) Scourge and Search for Death That Eludes Seekers (9:5-6)
      (6) Shape and Appearance Detailed of the Locusts (9:7-10)
      (7) Sovereign—Contrary to Nature for Locusts (9:11)
    f. Sixth Trumpet (9:13-21)
      (1) No Restriction on the Guardian Angels at the River (9:13-15)
      (2) No Resistance to the Oncoming Armies of the East (9:16-17)
      (3) No Resource and No Repentance for and by Mankind (9:18-21)
        A Third Killed by:
        (a) Fire
        (b) Smoke
        (c) Brimstone
E. Signs and Seventh Trumpet (10:1-11:19)
  1. Declaration by the Strong Angel (10:1-4)
    a. Seven Thunders Speak a Message (10:3)
    b. Sealed Message—Silence Imposed on John (10:4)
    c. Scroll in the Angel's Hand (10:1-2)
  2. Delay Over (10:5-7)
    a. Sworn by the Angel
    b. Seventh Trumpet about to Sound
    c. Secrets of the Mystery of God about to Be Revealed
  3. Demand Made upon the Scribe (10:8-11)
    a. Scroll

    c. Authority to Blaspheme for Three and One-half Years (13:5-6)

    d. Antagonism against the People of God (13:7-8)

    e. Apprising of the Signs and Situation (13:9-10)

  2. Second Beast from the Earth (13:11-18)

    a. His Deception and Devotion to the First Beast (13:11-13)

      (1) Diversity (13:11)

      (2) Demands (13:12)

      (3) Demonstrations (13:13)

    b. His Deeds and Decrees to Mankind (13:14-18)

      (1) Life to an Image (13:15)

      (2) Laws (13:15-16)

      (3) Label for All to Wear (13:16)

H. Safety and Suffering (14:1-20)

  1. Harpists Singing a New Song (14:1-5)

    a. Name of God on Their Foreheads (cf. 7:4) (14:1)

    b. Number of the Company Stated (cf. 7:4) (14:2-3)

    c. Nature of the Company (14:3-5)

      (1) Redeemed

      (2) Pure

      (3) Firstfruits

  2. Heralds—Three Angels Appear (14:6-13)

    a. Exhortation to All Mankind (14:6-7)

    b. Desolation of Babylon Declared (cf. 17:5,16; 18:1-8) (14:8)

    c. Proclamation to Men (14:9-11)

    d. Consolation to Those That Obey (14:12-13)

  3. Harvesters (14:14-20)

    a. A Cloud and Its Occupant—A Likeness to the Son of Man (14:14)

    b. A Cry and Its Order from an Angel from the Temple (14:15)

    c. A Condition and an Obligation to Gather the Harvest (14:16-18)

    d. A Crucible and Its Overflow That Resulted Therefrom (14:19-20)

I. Seven Vials (15:1-16:21)

  1. Introductory Movements (15:1-8)

    a. Seven Plagues to Fill Up the Wrath of God (15:1)

  c. Countryside Changes in Landscape and Pattern (16:20)

  d. Crushing Conclusion As Hail of More Than One Hundred Pounds Falls (16:21)

J. Seducing System Sentenced (17:1–18:24)

 1. Authority of the Angel to Show (17:1)

 2. Accusation of the Great Whore (17:2)

 3. Affirmation of the Fact (17:3)

 4. Adornment of the Woman (17:4)

 5. Advertisement on the Forehead (17:5)

 6. Astonishment of John at the Sight of Her (17:6)

 7. Answers Given to John by the Angel (17:7-18)

  a. Beast from the Pit Carried the Woman (17:7-8)

  b. Behavior of the Beast Who Was, Is Not, yet Is, with the Kings of the Earth (17:9-13)

  c. Battle of the Beast and His Allies with the Lamb Who Triumphs (17:14)

  d. Bitterness of the People against the Whore (17:15-17)

  e. Babylon of the Mysteries Identified (17:18)

 8. Acclamation of Victory (18:1-8)

  a. Condition of Babylon—Fallen and Devastated (18:1-2)

  b. Curse of Babylon—Her Doom and Excesses Noted (18:3)

  c. Call out of Babylon of God's People from Above (18:4)

  d. Cause and Effect in Babylon Remembered and Rewarded (18:5-6)

  e. Character of Babylon (18:7)

   (1) Pride

   (2) Plenty

   (3) Presumption

  f. Consequence for Babylon (18:8)

   (1) Death

   (2) Mourning

   (3) Famine

   (4) Fire

 9. Anguish of Her Votaries (18:9-19)

  a. Great Lamentation Involving So Many (18:9-18)

         (1) Mighty Men of the Earth Lament (18:9-10)

         (2) Merchants Join the Chorus—Loss of Trade (18:11-16)

         (3) Mariners Lament at the Destruction of the City (18:17-18)

    b. Great Loss Inflicted on So Many (18:9-19)

         (1) Mourners Cover a Large Cross-section of People (18:9-11)

         (2) Merchandise Covers Many Goods, Bodies, and Souls (18:12-14)

         (3) Manner of Life Covers Much Activity Therein (18:15-19)

  10. Angelic View (18:20-24)

    a. Rejoicing in Heaven At the Fall of Babylon (18:20)

    b. Retribution Inflicted upon Spiritual Iniquity (18:20-21)

    c. Ruin Indicated As Complete and Final (18:21-24)

         (1) No More City—Babylon Destroyed (18:21)

         (2) No More Crafts—The Arts Finished (18:22)

         (3) No More Candles—Babylon in Darkness (18:23)

         (4) No More Contented or Happy People There (18:23)

         (5) No Mention of Any Virtues to Be Found There (18:24)

K. Son and Savior (19:1-21)

  1. Alleluias—Four in Number Sound Forth (19:1,3-4,6)

  2. Appointment for the Marriage of the Lamb (19:7-10)

  3. Admonition for John to Worship God (19:10)

  4. Advent Focus on the Conquering Christ (19:11-16)

  5. Armies Follow Him from Heaven (19:14)

  6. Assignment from God to Smite and to Rule (19:15-16)

  7. Armageddon: Fall of the Gentile Powers and Dominion (19:17-21)

    a. Feast for the Fowls of the Air (19:17-18)

    b. Flower of the Federated Armies Amassed (19:19)

    c. Futile Foes of Christ in That Day (19:20-21)

    d. Final Features of That Battle (19:20-21)

L. Sequel Now Seen (20:1-15)

  1. Devil Restrained from all Activity (20:1-3)

      a. Power Demonstrated by the Angel of God (20:1)

      b. Period Declared for the Detention of Satan (20:2-3)

      c. Purpose Disclosed to Deceive No More (20:3)

      d. Prospect of Deliverance after the Millennium (20:3)

2. Dedicated Rewarded (20:4-6)

      a. Commitment to Christ beyond Question (20:4)

      b. Character to Be Established for All to See (20:4)

      c. Consolation as Servants of Christ Assured (20:5-6)

3. Deceiver Released (20:7-8)

      a. His Aim to Deceive the Nations against God (20:8)

      b. His Attractions Draw Sinners to Him Again (20:8)

      c. His Allies Demonstrate Their Loyalty to Him (20:8)

4. Destruction of the Rebels (20:9-10)

      a. Design to Destroy Both City and People (20:9)

      b. Doom Descends Suddenly upon Them (20:9)

      c. Devil Destined for Eternity in Lake of Fire (20:10)

5. Dead Raised (20:11-12)

      a. Person of the Judge, Christ Himself from Whom All Flee (20:11)

      b. Place of Judgment—The Great White Throne (20:11)

         (1) Not on Earth or in Heaven

         (2) No Glassy Sea or Worshipping Crowds

         (3) No Rainbow, Voices, Thunder, or Lightning

         (4) No Mountains, Rocks, or Dens

         (5) No Cover or Places to Hide or Escape

      c. People for Judgment—All Christ-Rejectors (20:12)

         (1) No Partiality

         (2) No Excuse

         (3) None Too Great or Small

      d. Plan for Judgment—According to Record of the Book Detailing Their Works (20:12)

      e. Passing of Judgment on All Present (20:13-15)

         (1) Deciding Factor—Not Found Written in the Book of Life

         (2) Deeds in Focus—According to Their Works

M. Satisfying Scenes (21:1–22:21)

    1. Revelation 21

a. New Creation (21:1-2)
   (1) New Heaven
   (2) New Earth
   (3) New Jerusalem
b. New Concept (21:3-8)
   (1) Fellowship of God with His People (21:3)
   (2) Freedom from the Frailty of Human Weakness (21:4)
   (3) Fidelity of God Providing for His Own (21:5-7)
   (4) Fire for All That Is Not of Christ (21:8)
c. New Consort (21:9-21)
   (1) Dignity
   (2) Descent
   (3) Description of the Bride
d. New Conditions (21:22-27)
   (1) Sanctuary—Person of God and the Temple (21:22)
   (2) Sun—Person of the Lamb, the Source of Light (21:23)
   (3) Saved—These Walk in Peace and Light (21:24)
   (4) Security That Is Unassailable There (21:25-27)

2. Revelation 22
   a. River of Life (22:1-3)
      (1) Clear and Fresh from the Throne of God (22:1)
      (2) Course Runs Freely through the Middle of the Street (22:2)
      (3) Crops of Fruits from a Great Variety Each Month (22:2)
      (4) Cure in the Foliage for the Healing of All (22:2)
      (5) Curse Finished Forever for All Within (22:3)
      (6) Contentment and Felicity for All There (22:3)
   b. Radiant Light (22:4-6)
      (1) The Sight—"They shall see his face" (22:4)
      (2) The Shining—"The Lord God giveth them light" (22:5)
      (3) The Sayings—"These sayings are faithful and true" (22:6)

c. Return of the Lord (22:7-14)
   (1) Retaining Prophetical Predictions a Source of Blessing (22:7)
   (2) Reaction Precipitated As John Saw and Heard (22:8)
   (3) Reproof and Request about Worship and Writings (22:9-10)
   (4) Remarks regarding Practices Habitual to All (22:11)
   (5) Reward for Personal Service Assured at His Coming (22:12)
   (6) Restitution Purposed—The Tree of Life Once Prohibited Now Available (22:13-14)
d. Responsibilities of Life (22:15-21)
   (1) Note the Adversaries—Servants of Satan (22:15)
   (2) Note the Angel—Sent to the Churches (22:16)
   (3) Note the Authority—"I Jesus" (22:16)
   (4) Note the Aim—Salvation for All Who Will Come (22:17)
   (5) Note the Additions and Subtractions Warned Against (22:18-19)
   (6) Note the Assurance and Reality (22:20-21)
      (a) Of the Promise
      (b) Of the Plea
      (c) Of the Benediction